How to Deliver a Great TED Talk

Presentation Secrets of the World's Best Speakers

Akash P. Karia

www.AkashKaria.com

PRAISE FOR "HOW TO DELIVER THE PERFECT TED TALK"

"Akash has **captured the best ideas, tools, and processes used by some of the best speakers and presenters in the world.** He has distilled them in to a step-by-step, easy-to-read guide that will help you discover, develop, and deliver presentations which help you stand out from the crowd."

- Michael Davis, Speaking CPR, Certified World Class Speaking Coach

"I was impressed with the range and extent of the very practical techniques and strategies that Akash Karia shares in this book. Through his extensive research he is able to provide lots of clear examples of exactly how to use them which makes a real difference if you are unfamiliar with the techniques. **Although it is directed at those preparing to give a TED talk it has step by step processes that can be used by anyone who wants to improve their presenting.."**

- Cath Daley, Presentation Specialist

"**Maybe one of the clearest books on presentations I've ever read.** Incredibly simple and easy to read but covering up a broad range of subjects. Full of practical tips, actual examples as well as personal experiences."

- Javier, Verified Amazon Reviewer

"**Hands on book to craft a mind-blowing memorable speech**"

-Tania de Winnie

"...this book contains **practical techniques with clear examples to help you become a more effective speaker and storyteller.**"

- Amey Hedge, Motivational Speaker and Corporate Trainer

"How to Deliver the Perfect TED Talk is **packed with practical ideas for delivering ANY presentation well!**"

-Cathy Bolger, Presentation Skills Instructor

"**A simple roadmap to a great TED talk.** As an accomplished Toastmaster, and instructor and committee member of TEDxYouth@FortWorth, I can say that this book hits all of key points to developing and delivering a dynamic and memorable TED Talk."

-Philip D. Mann, Toastmaster and TED enthusiast

CONTENTS

To Mum and Dad and my loving sister Bintee,
for always believing in me.

To my best friends,
Afshaan, Ali, Alfaz, Kok Lin and Salim,
for always being there for me.

To Chloe,
For helping make this a reality when I was stuck between dreaming
and doing.

SUCCESS PRINCIPLES FOR TED TALKS

If you've watched TED Talks (www.Ted.com), you've no doubt been inspired and enchanted by speeches by figures such as Sir Ken Robinson, Jill Bolte Taylor, Simon Sinek and Dan Pink.

What makes these TED talks so inspiring? What is the secret formula for creating a successful TED talk? And how can you use this formula to deliver your own powerful TED talk (or any other presentation or speech, for that matter)?

If you follow the guidelines and tools in this book, I guarantee that your audience will have no choice but to be wrapped up in your speeches and presentations.

I studied more than 200 of the most inspiring TED talks, analyzed each one line by line and discovered the common elements that make them successful. This book is the result of my rigorous research. In it, you'll discover tools that will help make you twice the speaker you are today in half the time.

This book is also based on the work of bestselling authors Chip and Dan Heath. In their groundbreaking book, *Made to Stick,* Chip and Dan Heath revealed six simple principles for creating memorable messages. In this book, I have taken Chip and Dan's work and applied it to creating powerfully persuasive presentations. I use their SUCCESS framework and draw on examples from TED talks to show how the success principles can be applied to public speaking.

You do not need to have read *Made to Stick* in order to get maximum value from this book (although I do recommend picking up a copy of the book). If you have already read Chip and Dan's book, you'll find this book a valuable addition to your library to help you create powerfully persuasive presentations and speeches.

According to Chip and Dan Heath, the SUCCESS formula for creating powerfully effective and memorable messages, which forms the foundation for the rest of the book, is:

SIMPLE

Any type of message – whether it's delivered in the form of an advertisement or a presentation – needs to be simple and clear to understand.

How do we apply this to presentations?

How do you know if your message is simple enough?

How do you make your message simple without dumbing it down?

Boil your presentation or speech down to one simple, core message. What one thing do you want your audience to remember by the end of the speech? You should be able to summarize this point in one sentence – and in words that even a child could understand. If you can do this, then your message meets the requirement for Simplicity.

Later on in this book, you will discover tools for making your message simple without dumbing it down.

UNEXPECTED

The best messages are shocking and say something unexpected.

In your presentations, the best way to grab your audience's attention is to do or say something unexpected. However, don't make this gimmicky (i.e., just for the sake of being unexpected). Make sure your "twist" is part of your message. One way of doing this is to provide shocking facts/statistics. For example, if you were giving a presentation on healthy eating choices, instead of saying, "Popcorn is very unhealthy!" you could say, "One bag of popcorn is as unhealthy as *a whole day's worth of fatty foods!*" This latter statement would shock your listeners and would be more memorable than the general statement about popcorn being unhealthy.

But what if you are delivering presentations that are boring in nature and contain absolutely zero shocking facts or twists?

Later in the book, you will learn how to take boring messages – even the ones that seem as though they have nothing shocking or unexpected – and turn them into powerful messages that contain the element of "unexpectedness."

CONCRETE

According to *Made to Stick*, the best messages are concrete rather than vague.

What does this mean for your presentations?

It means that you should avoid vague language. Provide specific, clear details. Instead of saying "a few months ago," say, "On March 19, 2011.☐ Instead of saying, "eat healthy," say, "make a commitment to never eat at McDonald's."

Later in the book, you will pick up more techniques on how to make your presentation more concrete.

CREDIBLE

The most effective messages are credible and believable.

So, how do you create credible presentations?

How do you build your credibility without seeming as though you're flaunting your achievements?

One strategy is to talk about things where you have an expertise. In other words, if you're speaking about "How to Be a Millionaire in 10 Days," make sure you're not broke. Make sure you live the message you preach.

Later on in the book, you'll learn how to borrow credibility from third-party sources.

EMOTIONAL

Advertisements and presentations that engage people's emotions will be memorable and effective.

How can you engage people's emotions even when giving boring, technical presentations?

One way is to engage people's emotions by telling them a story. In Chapter 21, you'll discover the five elements of great stories and how to use stories to engage people's emotions ... even when delivering standard, boring business presentations. You will also learn three very specific tools for adding humor into your speech.

STORY

The best messages use stories. Stories are a very powerful way of engaging people's emotions. You'll learn about the role of stories in presentations and you'll discover ways to add stories to make your presentations irresistible to your audience!

IN A NUTSHELL

There you have it, the SUCCESs checklist for sticky presentations:

- Simple
- Unexpected
- Concrete
- Credible
- Stories

Those are the six elements of great presentations, and by the end of this book, you'll have picked up over 100 very specific tools on presentation structure, delivery and content that you can use in your very next presentation to make it a roaring SUCCESS!

PART 1:

SIMPLE

Great presentations are simple and easy to understand. In this section we explore how to make your presentation simple without dumbing it down.

More specifically, by the end of this section you will know how to create simple yet effective presentations. You will learn:

- How to find your core message
- How to create your Power Phrase
- Rhetorical techniques to make your Power Phrase memorable
- The simple ABC-C structure for presentations
- Three opening mistakes to avoid
- Five Opening Gambits to create an attention-grabbing opening
- How to make your structure clear using a Roadmap
- Ten anchors to make your presentation memorable
- How to craft a compelling conclusion

Chapter One

HOW TO FIND YOUR CORE MESSAGE

The first step in creating a powerful TED presentation is to find a message you are passionate about. If you were given only 18 minutes to share your message with the world, what message would you share?

I have a poster with a powerful quote stuck on my bedroom wall. It's a quote that resonated with me the moment I read it. The quote is by Mark Brown, the Toastmasters International 1995 World Champion of Public Speaking:

> "Your life tells a story and there is someone out there who needs to hear it. You may think your story is not sensational, but it does not have to be sensational it just has to be sincere. If your audience can relate to you and your experiences, and chances are they will, then you need to tell them what you have been through, share your life, share your love and share your message with the world."

Even though I don't know you, I believe that you have a message that you need to share with the world. You have a story that can help others and it's your duty to share it.

If you still haven't found your story and your message, ask yourself: "What transformative experience have I gone through that can help others? What knowledge do I have that can make life easier for others? If I were to die today and had to leave my son/daughter/niece/nephew with only one message about living life, what message would I leave them with?"

TED speakers are people who are passionate about their messages. For example, brain researcher Dr. Jill Bolte Taylor (AkashKaria.com/Jill) shared on the TED stage the lesson she learned when a blood vessel exploded in the left half of her brain. Andy Puddicombe (AkashKaria.com/Andy) who left college midway through a sports science degree to become a monk, shared with his audience the importance of taking 10 minutes every day to focus on the present moment. Simon Sinek, (AkashKaria.com/Simon), who dedicated his career to studying successful organizations and leaders, delivered one of the most popular TED talks ever on how great leaders inspire action.

It doesn't matter what topic you choose. Topics on the TED stage have ranged from "10 things you didn't know about orgasm" to "how to tie your shoes" to "how to spot a liar." While the topics on the TED stage may be diverse, there is a commonality among all the speakers. They don't just give speeches – they open themselves up to the world and share their insights and experiences.

Find a message you are passionate about and which drives you. If you have a message that you genuinely believe in, delivering your speech will be easy because the passion will fuel your excitement. You won't have to fake a smile or rehearse your body language because your enthusiasm will guide your delivery.

Finding your message requires you to search inside yourself. The process can take anywhere from a couple of minutes to a couple of weeks. However, once you have found the story or experience you would like to share with your audience, the most important thing you must do is distill it into a core message. You should be able to write out the answer to the following question in less than 10 words:

If your audience was to forget everything else that you said, what is the one single thing that you would want them to remember?

For example, the core message of Simon Sinek's popular TED talk, "How great leaders inspire action," was the phrase "Start with why." Can you distill your core message down into a short and memorable sentence?

Finding the core of a message is about forced prioritization rather than "dumbing-down." You may have a lot of ideas you want to share with your audience, but you should strip away all the unnecessary ideas. You should even get rid of all the ideas that aren't *crucial* — aren't the *most important thing* that the audience should know.

Identifying and writing down your core message has two key benefits:

- It **helps you decide what to keep and what to throw out**. If you have an interesting story, statistic or chart, you should include it only if it helps explain your core message. If it doesn't, save it for another speech.

- It **helps the audience remember and understand** your presentation. Once you've stripped away all the unnecessary details, the audience gets the benefit of hearing a focused, simple and clear talk. When they leave, they'll remember you and your core message. You'll have made an impact.

As an example of "finding the core," let us examine an important idea from Bill Clinton's 1992 political campaign.

IT'S THE ECONOMY, STUPID

A political campaign is a war zone for hundreds of political issues: budget and spending, civil rights, drug policy, energy policy, foreign policy, health care, immigration, jobs and unemployment, national security, social security, tax policy. The list goes on and on.

With so many key issues at stake, is it possible for a political campaign to find *one single core message?*

In the 1992 U.S. election, Bill Clinton's political campaign did just that when they came up with the following slogan: *"It's the economy, stupid!"* Clinton's core message was that he was the guy who was going to get the economy back into shape. The Clinton campaign realized that while all the other issues were important ones, the most important one was to kick-start the economy. They began focusing all their efforts on promoting the core message – "It's the economy, stupid!" – because that was the most important issue on American voters' minds.

If Bill Clinton's campaign can be narrowed down into one core message, then your presentation certainly can too.

IN A NUTSHELL

- Finding your core message is about forced prioritization. If your audience was to forget everything else that you said, what is the one single thing that you would want them to remember?

- Write out your core message on a piece of paper in less than 20 words

- Your core message will help you decide what to include and what to discard. Ruthlessly cut out anything that is not directly related to the core message. The result will be a highly focused speech which the audience will remember and thank you for.

Chapter Two

CREATING A REPEATABLE POWER PHRASE

By the time your audience leaves your presentation, they've forgotten 20% of what you said. The following day, they've forgotten 50% of your message. Within four days, they've lost 80% of your message. These are disheartening statistics.

How do you make your presentation memorable?

How do you make your core message sticky?

How do you make sure your message doesn't go in one ear and out the other?

One of the best ways to ensure your message gets remembered and repeated is to boil your core message down into a single, catchy phrase that you can repeat several times throughout the presentation. This phrase is called a Power Phrase.

For example, consider Martin Luther King's "I Have a Dream" speech. His power phrase was "I have a dream." It is a phrase that has withstood the test of time.

One important thing about your Power Phrase is that it should be less than 10 words. If it's any longer, it will be too long to remember.

There are several rhetorical devices you can use to make your Power Phrase catchy.

CONTRAST

Use contrast to make your phrase catchy. Consider pairing opposite ideas together to make your phrase memorable. For example, look at the following pairing of opposites:

"It is our **light**, not our **darkness** that most frightens us."
Marianne Williamson

"No one **rises** to **low** expectations."
John Leslie Brown

"Who can you count **in** and who should you count **out**?"
John Leslie Brown

"The solution is not to do more of the wrong things, to entice people with a **sweeter carrot**, or threaten them with a **sharper stick**. We need a whole new approach."
Dan Pink

"People **don't buy** what you do, **they buy** why you do it."
Simon Sinek

CHIASMUS

Chiasmus is a rhetorical device in which the order of the words in the second of two paired phrases is the reverse of the order in the first. For example:

"Ask not what **your country** can do for **you** – ask what **you** can do for **your country**"
John F. Kennedy

"When the **going** gets **tough**, the **tough** gets **going**"

"We don't **mistrust each other** because we're **armed**; we're **armed** because we **mistrust each other**."
Ronald Reagan

"People the world over have always been more impressed by the **power** of our **example** than by the **example** of our **power**." *Bill Clinton*

RHYME

In his excellent book on persuasion, "YES: 50 Secrets from the Science of Persuasion," Dr. Robert Cialdini writes that "rhyme can make your influence climb." It turns out that people perceive rhyming statements as being truer than non-rhyming statements. Plus, rhyming statements are easier to remember.

"Trust is a must."
Ryan Avery, 2012 Toastmasters World Champion of Public Speaking

"What the mind of man can conceive and believe, it can achieve"
Napoleon Hill

ALLITERATION

Alliteration is the repetition of an initial consonant sound. Consider the following Power Phrase, which makes great use of alliteration:

"I have a dream that my four little children will one day live in a nation where they will not be judged by the color of their skin, but by the content of their character."
Martin Luther King

"If you can dream it, you can do it"
Walt Disney

"The solution is not to do more of the wrong things, to entice people with a sweeter carrot, or threaten them with a sharper stick. We need a whole new approach."
Dan Pink

"People don't buy what you do, they buy why you do it."
Simon Sinek

IN A NUTSHELL

- Turn your core message into a short, repeatable Power Phrase
- Use one or a combination of the following rhetorical techniques to make your Power Phrase memorable:
    - Contrast
    - Chiasmus
    - Rhyme
    - Alliteration

Chapter Three

THE ABC-C FORMULA FOR POWERFUL PRESENTATIONS

The SUCCESS principles state that your presentation needs to be simple and easy to understand. This is achieved by having a clear structure.

The best presentations follow the ABC-C structure.

What is the ABC-C structure?

A – ATTENTION-GRABBING OPENING

Your speech needs to have an attention-grabbing opening. If you don't grab your audience's attention within the first 30 seconds of your speech, they're going to tune out of your presentation.

Unfortunately, most presentations today have very boring, predictable openings that turn audience members off:

> "Hi. My name is ABC. It's a pleasure to be here on such an important occasion. So, before I begin, I'd like to introduce my

organization to you. Our company was founded in 1959 by Mr. XYZ, after which it was acquired by …"

Have you ever been bored by such an opening?

Have *you* ever bored your audience with such an opening?

In the following chapter, you'll learn how to avoid boring openings and you'll pick up five specific tools that you can use to create openings that immediately capture your audience's attention. You'll also learn how *not* to open so that you can avoid the mistakes most other speakers make.

B – BODY

The next part of your presentation is the body.

This is where you make your main arguments and points. Later in the book, you'll pick up specific tools on how to make the body of your speech compelling and persuasive.

C – CONCLUSION

Every speech needs a clear conclusion.

Unfortunately, I've seen too many speakers abruptly end their speeches with the terrible phrase, "That's the end of my presentation." Later in the book, you'll learn exactly how to conclude your speech so that you leave a positive final impression on your audience.

C – CLEAR CALL TO ACTION

Every speech and presentation needs to have a clear call to action.

The call to action makes it clear what you want your audience members to do differently as a result of having listened to your presentation. Later in the book, you'll learn about the importance of including a clear "next step" that your audiences can take after having listened to your presentation.

Every presentation needs to have a clear opening, body, conclusion and call to action. There are other structures that you can use, such as the "Problem/Solution" structure, "Chronological" structure, "Step-by-Step" structure and the "Feature-Benefits" structure, but all of them have an attention-grabbing opening, body, conclusion and clear call to action.

PROBLEM/SOLUTION

The problem/solution structure is a powerful speech structure. You open with an attention-grabbing opening which highlights the problem. You then transition into the body of the speech where you establish the extent of the problem and describe the consequences of not solving it.

Once you've built up enough pain and have your audience members craving a solution, you present your solution. You explain how it will help alleviate the pain and offer the advantages of the solution.

In your conclusion, you restate the problem and the consequences of not solving it. You remind them of the advantages of your solution and end with a clear call to action urging audience members to support your solution.

In his fascinating TED talk (AkashKaria.com/Ken), Sir Ken Robinson uses a loose version of the problem/solution structure. For example, most of his speech focuses on the problem with the current educational system. Here's a paragraph from the first half of his speech:

> "...it's education that's meant to take us into this future that we can't grasp. If you think of it, children starting school this year will be retiring in 2065. Nobody has a clue - despite all the expertise that's been on parade for the past four days - what the world will look like in five years' time. And yet we're meant to be educating them for it."

Only after having completely explained the problem does Sir Ken present the solution. In your speeches and presentations, make you sure you never present the solution without first having built up the pain/problem. People don't care about a solution unless the pain is excruciating enough for them to feel an urgent need to find a cure.

CHRONOLOGICAL

The chronological speech structure is very simple. You organize and explain events according to time, starting with the oldest. For example, if you were giving a presentation about how marketing has changed over time, you might start talking about what marketing was like 20 years ago. You would then talk about how marketing is done now. And you would end with your prediction of how marketing will change in the future. It's a simple, easy to understand speech structure.

STEP-BY-STEP

Closely related to the chronological speech structure is the step-by-step structure. In this speech structure, you logically walk your audience through the different steps towards an event. For example, in her TED talk on domestic violence (AkashKaria.com/Leslie), Leslie Morgan Steiner walks her audience through the different stages in a domestic violence relationship:

> "I didn't know that the first stage in any domestic violence relationship is to seduce and charm the victim...I also didn't know that the second step is to isolate the victim...The next step in the domestic violence pattern is to introduce the threat of violence and see how she reacts..."

Leslie uses numbering to make her steps clear ("first step, second step"). This makes her sequence very clear. After introducing each step, Leslie tells her personal story to explain each step (e.g., how her ex-husband seduced her, isolated her and then introduced the threat of violence to see how she reacted). The result is a very powerful and moving speech.

If you have several points in your speech, consider numbering them to make your speech flow logically.

FEATURES/BENEFITS

This is a great presentation structure if you're talking about a product or a service. Steve Jobs was a master at using this structure. While most presenters would focus only on the features of the product, Steve Jobs would also sell the benefits. He would make it absolutely clear how the audience would benefit from a particular feature of his product. For example, when he introduced iTunes movie rentals, he clearly explained the benefits of rentals by saying:

> "We've never offered a rental model in music because people want to own their music. You listen to your favorite songs

25

thousands of times in your life. But most of us watch movies once, maybe a few times. And renting is a great way to do it. **It's less expensive, doesn't take up space on our hard drive…"**

A client who I was coaching once asked me, "Can't the audience figure out the benefits if we just give them the features? I don't want to treat the audience as though they're dumb!"

It's a good question. No, the audience isn't dumb. However, don't make them think too hard about the benefits. They may not always make the connection between the features and the benefits. Either the connection may not be clear or they may be too lazy to make it.

Also, when your audience walks away from your presentation, they will most likely forget many of the features. If you only list out the features, they'll forget most of what you tell them. However, they *will* remember the benefits. So make sure you clearly state the benefit of each and every feature. People buy a product or service because of the benefits it offers them, not because of the features, so make sure you spend plenty of time elaborating the benefits.

You may choose to go with one of the structures listed in this chapter or some other structure that suits your needs much better. However, no matter which structure you choose, make sure that it has an attention-grabbing opening, with a clear body and a compelling conclusion with a clear next step for your audience to take.

IN A NUTSHELL

- Great presentations require a simple easy-to-follow structure
- Structures you can use are:
    - Problem/Solution
    - Chronological
    - Step-by-Step
    - Features/Benefits
- No matter which structure you use, all presentations need to contain an Attention-grabbing opening, Body, Conclusion and Clear call to action (ABC-C)

Chapter Four

CREATING AN ATTENTION-GRABBING OPENING

You should spend time writing and rewriting your opening because it's one of the two most important parts of your speech or presentation (the other part being the closing).

THE PRIMACY EFFECT

Primacy Effect: "Given a list of items to remember, we will tend to remember the first few things more than those things in the middle." –ChangingMinds.org

Because of our tendency to remember the things at the beginning of a list, speech or presentation, the opening of your speech is the most important part of the presentation.

The opening of your speech is important for several additional reasons. It gives you a chance to do the following:

- build rapport with the audience members,

- create a first impression will that determine how receptive or hostile your audience will be towards your speech,
- set the mood for the rest of the speech, and
- grab your audience's attention within the first 30 seconds, so that they don't mentally check out of your presentation

LESSONS FROM *"THE DARK KNIGHT,"* *"GOODFELLAS"* **AND** *"TWILIGHT"*

Think of the last great film that you watched. Many films begin slam-bang in the middle of a fight scene, a car chase, a bomb explosion or a bank robbery. The aim is to get you involved, interested and engaged right away. The blockbuster movie *"The Dark Knight"* begins in the middle of a bank heist.

Other movies aren't as dramatic and instead open with an unexpected or shocking statement that engages you straight away. Consider the opening line of *"GoodFellas"*: "As far back as I can remember, I always wanted to be a gangster."

Successful scriptwriters, movie producers and speechwriters know that the key to success is to throw the audience right into the middle of the story. Even fiction writers know that the first few lines of the book are among the most important ones – the audience will mentally tune in or out depending on how well you've managed to engage their attention right from the very beginning.

Consider the opening line from the phenomenal bestselling book *"Twilight"*:

> "I'd never given much thought to how I would die – though I'd never had reason enough in the last few months – but even if I had, I would not have imagined it like this."

The opening line shocks and leaves you wondering, *"Wow! What's happening? Why is she dying? How is she dying?"*

The purpose of the opening few lines of any speech, movie or book is to engage the audience straight away … to grab their attention from the outset.

How many speeches or presentations have you watched where the speaker managed to grab your interest from the first few lines that he spoke?

How many speakers have you heard whose openings made you think, "Wow, this is going to be really good"?

Now, consider, how good are *you* at creating compelling openings which reel your audience into your speech? If you feel that there's room for improvement, this chapter will be valuable for you. You will pick up tools you can use to arouse your audiences' interest and grab their attention from the beginning.

But first, let's discover the three opening mistakes that you should avoid:

1. BORING "ME-FOCUSED" OPENING

Unfortunately, too many speakers begin with boring "me-focused" openings that put their audiences to sleep.

Have you ever heard a speaker begin a presentation with an opening that sounds similar to this?

> "Good morning. Thank you very much for having me. My name is ABC and I am from Company XYZ. My company has been in existence for 150 years. We focus on providing out-of-the-box, customer-centered strategies that leverage our client's strengths

and empower them to achieve organic growth in this new economy."

How excited do you think audiences will be to learn the history, mission and values of your organization? Not very.

The key to giving great presentations is to make them not about the speaker but about the audience! Presentations are about the audience … not the speaker.

Therefore, your opening should be You-focused. It should let audience members know exactly what problems you can solve for them and what benefits you can give them!

2. OPENING WITH INSINCERE GRATITUDE

A fellow public speaking coach started his seminar in this manner. When he walked into the room, he began with:

> "Hi, thank you very much for having me today. I'm very pleased to be here, and I'd like to thank Mr. X for having invited me to conduct this workshop."

At this point, the coach looked us in the eye and said:

> "Okay, so how many of you expected me to say exactly what I just said … almost word for word?"

People began to laugh and everyone in the room raised their hands.

The point is simple: Almost everyone begins their speeches and presentations with a "thank you," using almost the same exact words.

If you're one of these presenters, then you're losing out on a great opportunity to differentiate yourself from everyone else. You're losing out on an opportunity to make a great first impression!

Even worse, many of your audience members might unconsciously label you as boring and uncreative, like every other speaker they've seen, and they'll mentally tune out of your presentation. Trying to bring these people back will be a challenge, and you'll be left with an uncomfortable room full of strangers who aren't really listening to what you're saying.

As you're about to discover, there are several techniques that you can use to capture your audience's attention and imagination straight away. However, before you come to those, let's first address a common objection that most people raise during my public speaking workshops: "Why shouldn't I thank people at the beginning? It's the polite thing to do!"

Most speakers, despite knowing the dangers of using a standard "thank you for having me here" opening, continue using it because they are under the false assumption that thanking people *must* be done at the beginning of their presentation.

There is nothing wrong with thanking your hosts and your audience members for having you, but it doesn't necessarily have to be done at the beginning. In fact, not only might you lose your audience with a canned "thank-you" opening, your gratitude may also be perceived as insincere. The fact is, because most speakers say "thank you" during their opening few lines, *your* "thank you" will sound no different ... it will be considered as an opening formality rather than a sincere expression of gratitude.

So, when is the best time to thank your audience and your hosts?

The best time to show your gratitude – both to your hosts and your audience – would be sometime *after* your first minute on stage, after you've established rapport with the audience.

For example, a fellow speaker who was given the opportunity to present a training seminar on leadership thanked his audience during the middle of his speech, when he said: "And by the way, talking about leadership, we can all agree that Jim *(the CEO)* has done a fantastic job of leading this company!" This unexpected comment during the middle of the speech sounded more sincere and honest than a canned "thank-you" beginning.

Another comedian who I witnessed thanked his audience a couple of minutes into his routine (after he had all of us laughing at his opening story) and said, "By the way, you guys are a great audience and it's really my privilege to be here today! See, last week I had this other audience who ..." and then he dived right into another joke.

The key point here is that you should avoid canned "thank-you" openings because you end up losing an important opportunity to distinguish yourself from most other speakers. Furthermore, you will lose your audience (after all, why should they listen if they already know what you're going to say?) and your gratitude may be perceived as insincere. Instead, thank your audience *after* you've established a connection with them using one of the five opening strategies you'll pick up later in the chapter.

Note: I do realize that there are some very formal situations where you simply *must* begin your speech by thanking your hosts. If that's the case, a short and simple "Thank you" will suffice, after which you can dive into a question or a story.

3. OPENING WITH A JOKE

"Should I open my presentation or speech with a joke?"

Ah, interesting question! Humor is a great way to form a bond with the audience. A humorous speaker immediately gets the goodwill of the audience and is perceived as a more likeable speaker than someone with little or no humor.

However, my personal suggestion would be to avoid opening with a joke for two reasons:

- **Jokes from a joke book don't impress anyone:** If you use a joke that you've read in a joke book or on the Internet, there's the danger that the audience might have heard it before. Immediately, you'll be labeled as unoriginal and the audience will doubt the authenticity of the rest of your presentation.

- **Jokes might detract from your main message**. I've seen some presenters open with a joke that was completely unrelated to the main point the presenter was trying to make. In an attempt to be funny, most presenters go out of their way to include jokes that take attention away from their main message. After all, it is very difficult to find a joke directly related to the point you're trying to prove. Bottom line: Don't open with a joke that has nothing to do with your presentation!

- **Most people can't tell jokes as well as they think they can**. A joke requires expert timing and great use of facial expressions, both of which most speakers lack. This results in a "bombed joke" and creates an uncomfortable silence in the room. If you're the victim of an opening joke that falls flat on its face, this may negatively affect your confidence throughout the rest of the speech.

However, if you are a humorous speaker, you *may* want to open with a humorous story (one which is related to your message). The reason a humorous story works is because it's your personal story, so no one in the audience has heard it before. In addition, there's no pressure on you to be funny as there is when you are telling a joke. Finally, stories are intriguing, so they will help you capture the attention of your audience.

FIVE BRILLIANT WAYS TO START YOUR NEXT PRESENTATION

After having studied more than 200 TED talks, I have found that there are five ways you can open your speech that are proven to capture your audience's attention:

1. START WITH A STORY

The best speakers are master storytellers. They tell touching tales, using compelling stories as a means to solidify their message. A well-told story will always be remembered.

A story is a great way to open your speech, but it also works just as well as a closer. In fact, according to Bill Gove, the first president of the National Speakers Association, the essence of public speaking is to "tell a story, [and] make a point."

In her popular TED talk on the power of introverts (AkashKaria.com/Susan), Susan Cain hooked her audience into her speech by immediately diving into a personal story:

> "When I was nine years old I went off to summer camp for the first time. And my mother packed me a suitcase full of books, which to me seemed like a perfectly natural thing to do. Because in my family, reading was the primary group activity. And this might sound antisocial to you, but for us it was really just a

different way of being social. You have the animal warmth of your family sitting right next to you, but you are also free to go roaming around the adventure-land inside your own mind. And I had this idea that camp was going to be just like this, but better...”

See, you're curious to find out more about her camping experience, aren't you?

The reason a story is a superb opening strategy is because:

- **Stories captivate people**: Everyone loves a good story, so starting with a story will capture your audience's attention. The moment you begin with a story, your audience will have no choice but to tune in.

- **Stories create connections between the listeners and the speaker**: A personal story will arouse emotions in the listeners. Studies have shown that our brains cannot tell the difference between "real" events and imagined events. Therefore, when you tell a story, your audience will imagine it and "feel" the same emotions that you're describing. Your story will not be forgotten because your audience will "experience" it rather than just hear it.

- **Stories are memorable**: We are hard-wired to learn through stories. Scientific research has shown that we make sense of the world through stories. People even view their lives as a story, with a beginning, a middle and an end, and with each new experience being regarded as a "new chapter" in their lives. Because of this natural hard-wiring, we may forget statistics and fancy charts, but we will always remember a good story.

Since stories are such an important tool in effective communication, you will discover the essentials of great storytelling in a later chapter. These secrets will allow you to become a master storyteller and speaker, entertaining your friends as well as your audiences.

2. USE QUESTIONS TO CREATE KNOWLEDGE GAPS

Starting with a question creates a knowledge gap: *a gap between what the listeners know and what they don't know.* This gap creates curiosity because people are hard-wired with a desire to fill knowledge gaps.

For example, starting with a question such as "What's the number one reason that most people fail to advance in their careers, working harder and longer, yet never achieving their dreams?" gets your audience thinking and starting to formulate their answers. You've got them hooked!

In his TED talk, Simon Sinek (AkashKaria.com/Simon) began his speech with a series of powerful questions:

> "How do you explain when things don't go as we assume? Or better, how do you explain when others are able to achieve things that seem to defy all of the assumptions? For example: Why is Apple so innovative? Year after year, after year, after year, they're more innovative than all their competition. And yet, they're just a computer company. They're just like everyone else. They have the same access to the same talent, the same agencies, the same consultants, the same media. Then why is it that they seem to have something different? Why is it that Martin Luther King led the Civil Rights Movement? He wasn't the only man who suffered a pre-civil rights America. And he certainly wasn't the only great orator of the day. Why him? And why is it that the

38

Wright brothers were able to figure out control-powered, manned flight when there were certainly other teams who were better qualified, better funded, and they achieve powered man flight, and the Wright brothers beat them to it. There's something else at play here."

One important thing to note about asking questions is you must make sure that you *pause after your question* so that the audience has enough time to reflect on your question. If you don't pause after your questions, you'll be trampling over their thoughts and they won't pay attention to what you're saying.

The final benefit of opening with a question is that it allows you to create a connection with the audience. For example, in his winning speech at the Toastmasters International World Championship of Public Speaking, Darren LaCroix opened with the following question:

> "Can you remember a moment when a brilliant idea flashed into your head?" – Darren LaCroix, 2001 World Champion of Public Speaking

If you were in this audience, you would naturally think to yourself, "Yes! I know what you're talking about!"

When your audience can relate to a question you've asked, you've successfully created a connection

In your next presentation, open with a question that the audience can relate to or with a question that creates a knowledge gap and creates curiosity in your listeners. Once you do this, your listeners will be hooked onto your every word!

You can deliver the perfect opening by first starting with a question that builds curiosity, and then filling that knowledge gap by telling a story that illustrates the main point of your speech.

For example, let us say that you opened with the following question:

> "What's the number one reason that most people fail to advance in their careers, working harder and longer, yet never achieving their dreams?"

At this point, if you were an average speaker, you could immediately reveal your answer and tell the audience, *"The number one reason most people fail is because they do not set goals for themselves."*

However, as a reader of this book, you can do something even better. You can let the listeners *discover* the answer rather than simply handing it to them. You can prolong their curiosity by diving into a story that illustrates your point. For example, after asking your opening question, you could tell the story of your friend Jerry, who worked long hours each night at the office but never achieved any success. You can then reveal how Jerry discovered the power of goal-setting and went on to become vice president of his company.

In this way, instead of simply handing your answer to your audience, you've let them discover it for themselves through Jerry's story. You've successfully captured your audience's interest, and you've made an impact because they'll remember Jerry's story.

So, create a knowledge gap using a question and then fill the gap using a compelling story.

3. QUOTABLE QUOTES

Would you like to add credibility to your speech?

Would you build the credibility of your message by borrowing credibility from a third-party source?

Consider opening with a quote.

A short quote that illustrates your main point will create support for your speech. For example, if you are giving a speech about the need to keep things simple, then you could borrow Einstein's credibility by starting like this:

> Einstein said, "Imagination is more important ... than knowledge!"

However, here are a few pointers to keep in mind when choosing your quotes:

- **Shorter is sweeter:** The shorter your quote, the greater the impact. A long quote will end up boring your audience.

- **Make sure it's relevant**: Make sure the quote is relevant to your main point, and relevant for the atmosphere. A playful quotation from Homer Simpson may not be appropriate during a tear-filled funeral.

- **Check the source!** Check the source's credibility. Don't quote Hitler if you're delivering a speech about the importance of ethics!

- **Quote a well-known authority:** Quoting your high school friend may please your friend, but it's not going to earn you extra points from the audience. Quote someone who is familiar to everyone in the audience.

- **Choose a quote that hasn't been overused.** Some quotes have been overused so much that audience members are tired of listening to them. Try to use a quote that audience members may not have heard before.

For example, in his speech for the 2003 Toastmasters International World Championship of Public Speaking, when he talked about the importance of dreaming, Jim Key used a quote by Martin Luther King. However, instead of going with Dr. King's overused "I have a dream" quote, Jim Key used another one which also fit perfectly into his speech:

"Martin Luther King, one of the greatest dreamers of our age said, "The time is always right to do what is right!", which means that if it was right for us to dream as children, it's also right for us to dream as adults."

4. INTERESTING/STARTLING STATEMENT

Dale Carnegie said, "Begin with something interesting in your first sentence. Not the second. Not the third. The First! F-I-R-S-T! First!"

You can immediately differentiate yourself and your topic from most other speakers by shocking your listeners with a startling statement. For example, if you're talking about the importance of avoiding fast food, you could start with the following statement:

"If you eat a McDonald's quarter pounder with cheese, you'll instantly gain almost half a pound of weight!"

For a statement to be shocking, it has to be something that is not common knowledge. When you provide a fact that most people are unaware of, you've instantly added value to their lives and made a positive impression on them.

You don't necessarily have to use shocking statements to get people to listen. An intriguing statement can do an equally good job. For example:

> "In 1989, when I was graduating from college, my professor told me something which changed my life ... and it could change yours too."

The above statement intrigues the listeners. It causes them to wonder, "What did your professor say? How did it change your life? And how can it change my life?"

Intriguing statements create a mystery. They create knowledge gaps that the audience feels compelled to fill.

If you can find an interesting or startling statement that backs up your speech's core message, be sure to open with it and you'll have your listeners wrapped up in your presentation.

5. CALL-BACK

A call-back is when you refer back to something that happened before or during the event. For example, in his TED talk, Sir Ken Robinson (AkashKaria.com/Ken) called back to the presentations that had taken place before his. He said:

> "There have been three themes, haven't there, running through the conference, which are relevant to what I want to talk about. One is the extraordinary evidence of human creativity in all of the presentations that we've had and in all of the people here. Just the variety of it and the range of it. The second is that it's put us in a place where we have no idea what's going to happen, in terms of the future..."

Later in the speech, he called back to an event that had taken place the night before:

"And the third part of this is that we've all agreed, nonetheless, on the really extraordinary capacities that children have -- their capacities for innovation. I mean, Sirena last night was a marvel, wasn't she? Just seeing what she could do. And she's exceptional, but I think she's not, so to speak, exceptional in the whole of childhood. What you have there is a person of extraordinary dedication who found a talent. And my contention is, all kids have tremendous talents."

Calling back to earlier presentations gives Ken Robinson's speech a personalized feel. It lets the audience members know that the speech is customized for them, as opposed to being an off-the-shelf speech.

In your speeches and presentations, you can call back to previous speakers or to events that took place before you spoke.

*

Opening with a story, question, quote, interesting/startling statement or call-back of an earlier event is just one aspect of creating a powerful opening. After opening with one of the five proven openers, you may sometimes need to include a Big Promise, a Pain Statement and a Roadmap. Let's start with the Big Promise:

INCLUDE A BIG PROMISE

If you've ever stayed up late at night watching infomercials that are selling electronic ab belts, you've probably heard some of these phrases:

- Now you can get rock-hard abs…with no sweat!
- Lose 4 inches in 30 days – Guaranteed!

- 30% More Effective than Normal Exercise

The above phrases are the **Big Promises** of electronic ab belts. The electronic ab belts work on the basis that the electronic signals from the belt provides muscle stimulation…hence, you can sit around and just "watch the fat melt away" – without breaking a sweat! As a result of these Big Promises, the electronic ab belts became a "must-have" (I will admit that after hearing these Big Promises, I wanted one too!). However, in 2002, the U.S. Federal Trade Commission charged the three best-selling electronic ab belts with making false claims such as the ones listed above.

The Big Promise can be very effective in winning people's time, attention and money. Hopefully you also realize how easy it is to abuse the Big Promise, and I hope that you'll make sure your Big Promises are never Empty Promises.

In the business world, there are lots of examples of companies that are using the Big Promise ethically and honestly. Here are a few:

RYANAIR: Ryanair's Lowest Fare Guarantee – Or We Pay You Double The Difference

FACEBOOK: Facebook helps you connect and share with the people in your lives

WALMART: Save money. Live better.

So, what does all this have to do with creative powerfully persuasive presentations?

Simply, make sure that your presentation offers your audience members a Big Promise.

What is the Big Promise of your presentation? What benefit does your presentation offer your audience? Why should they listen to you? What's in it for them?

Give your audience members such a compelling reason to listen to your speech that they have no choice but to be curious and excited about what you have to offer them.

Create the most compelling Big Promise that you possibly can and put it somewhere near the beginning of your presentation.

For example, during my workshops on public speaking skills, I offer the participants the following Big Promise:

> "By the end of this half-day workshop, you will have the tools and techniques to become a powerfully persuasive speaker. If you apply the techniques you learn today, I almost guarantee that you'll walk away twice as good as when you first came in. The five tools you're going to pick up today will shave years off your learning curve. Plus, you'll become the kind of confident speaker who keeps their audiences engaged, excited and entertained! The first tool…"

The Big Promise always has audience members leaning in closer, wanting to hear more. When you use the Big Promise in your presentations, your audience won't be able to wait to hear what you have to say!

Your Big Promise doesn't need to be as long and as elaborate as mine. It could be just a sentence or two. For example, if you're pitching a new idea to your boss, you could say:

> "In this presentation, we're going to discuss ways our business can tap into an untapped market that's worth $400 million!"

Here's another example. If you're a sales trainer, you could start your seminar with:

> "Over the next 20 minutes, you're going to pick up tools on how to double your sales and triple your revenue"

When creating your Big Promise, there are several things to keep in mind:

- **Answer the WIIFM Question:** At the beginning of every presentation or speech, audience members are asking themselves, "WIIFM: What's in it for me?" Make sure your Big Promise gives your audience members a compelling reason to listen to the rest of your presentation.

- **Include Your Biggest Benefits in the Big Promise:** What are the biggest benefits your audience members will gain from listening to you? Include the top three biggest benefits in your Big Promise.

- **Cover the EDGE Benefits:** Audience members are motivated by different things. Some are motivated by the prospect of making more money. Others are motivated by having more time. Others want more enjoyment.

  In his book, *World Class Speaking,* Craig Valentine talks about the EDGE Benefits. He classifies the different types of benefits that motivate audience members into the acronym EDGE, which stands for:

  - **Esteem More:** More confidence
  - **Do More:** Doing more in less time, achieving more
  - **Gain More:** Gaining more money, gaining more time

- **Enjoy More:** Having more pleasure, more fun, more enjoyment, more happiness

If you can include at least one benefit from each of the EDGE elements, you're likely to have covered the needs of all your audience members.

- **Make Your Benefits Specific:** Make your benefits as specific as possible. Instead of saying, "You'll sell more," say, "You'll double your sales." Instead of saying, "You'll be a better speaker," say, "You'll become twice as good as when you first came in." Instead of saying, "You'll lose weight and look great," say, "You'll melt away all the fat and have washboard abs." Specifics create excitement because they paint a clear picture of the benefits in your audience's minds.

- **Make Sure You Can Deliver on Your Big Promise:** Make sure you don't make any Empty Promises, otherwise your audience will feel cheated and manipulated. I once saw a speaker who, at the beginning of his presentation, promised that he would reveal to us a formula that would guarantee that we would win more than 95% of the time when playing poker against our friends. As a poker player, I was tremendously excited to hear this formula. Maybe it was a new mathematical strategy that would help me win more money? Unfortunately, later on during the presentation, the speaker said: "There is no formula that will win 95% of the time." It was a huge disappointment and I felt cheated. Although the speaker did make some other very good points about how to calculate poker odds, I walked away from the speech feeling manipulated and disappointed.

Note: Your Big Promise doesn't always have to be explicit. It can be implicit. Let me explain. Consider Simon Sinek's TED talk (AkashKaria.com/Simon) opening again:

> "How do you explain when things don't go as we assume? Or better, how do you explain when others are able to achieve things that seem to defy all of the assumptions? For example: Why is Apple so innovative? Year after year, after year, after year, they're more innovative than all their competition."

Simon doesn't state explicitly that his audience will learn why some people and companies seem to achieve success when others do not. Instead, it is *implied* through the questions he asks.

If you're unable to make an explicit Big Promise, use questions to make an implicit Big Promise to make the audience curious and hungry for your information.

INLCUDE A PAIN STATEMENT

People are motivated by two things:

1. **Gaining Pleasure** (i.e. Benefits): People take action because they gain some benefit out of the action. They gain happiness, confidence, wealth, etc. In your presentation, the Big Promise provides your audience members with compelling benefits that motivate your audience members to listen to you.

2. **Avoiding Pain and Loss**: People are motivated by avoiding pain and loss. In fact, research shows that people are more motivated to avoid loss than they are to gain benefit of an equal amount.

Thus, apart from the Big Promise, your presentation opening also needs to highlight the pain your audience members currently are suffering from. You need to insert a short Pain Statement after your Big Promise to motivate your audience to listen to you by pointing out what they currently are losing out on.

For example, let's take some Big Promises and attach short Pain Statements *(in italics)* to each one to see how they would look:

> "Over the next 15 minutes, we're going to discuss ways our business can tap into an untapped market that could increase our revenue by 500%! *By ignoring this untapped market, we're losing out on $400 million worth of annual revenue!*"

Here's another example:

> "Over the next 20 minutes, you're going to pick up tools on how to double your sales and triple your revenue. *Every day that you're not using these techniques, you're losing out on thousands of dollars in income.*"

In my communication skills workshops and seminars, I magnify the pain by asking audience members to think about the opportunities that they've missed out on:

> "Great communication skills are essential to your success in business. Think about it: *How many times has your big idea been shot down because you lacked the tools to persuade the key decision makers? How often have you seen other colleagues get promoted up the corporate ladder faster than you – not because they were better businesspeople, but because they were more confident and eloquent speakers? How much potential income have you lost out on because you lacked the skills to close the sale?*"

By using these Pain Questions and Pain Statements, you make your audiences temporarily uncomfortable with the situation they're currently in … and when they get uncomfortable, they start looking for solutions to alleviate the pain. All you have to do in your presentation is to package your solution/idea as one that will help your audience remove that pain while moving them closer to their goals and dreams.

Now, some of you may be reading this and thinking, "I can't say that in my presentation! My boss would think me arrogant. This technique would never work for me."

It's true that it may not always be wise to include such an explicit pain statement. However, again, it is possible to include an *implicit* pain statement.

For example, Nick, a lawyer, came to me for presentation coaching because he had to give a talk to a group of bankers explaining the importance of following a new piece of banking legislation in Hong Kong. The bankers he was going to present to were busy people who were being forced by their bosses to attend Nick's talk. In other words, they were not interested in learning about the legislation because they didn't think it was important to their careers.

To grab the audience's attention and interest, Nick and I decided that it would be best to open with a short story which would highlight the pain the bankers would face if they *didn't* follow the legislation. So Nick began his presentation with a story of how a major bank in the U.S. had ignored a similar piece of legislation and as a result was fined hundreds of millions of dollars. Some of the organization's senior bankers were fired for not following the regulation.

With this opening, Nick had the full attention of all the bankers in the room because the story served as an implicit pain statement. It implicitly highlighted the consequences the audience would face if they didn't listen to him. Nick then softened his approach and carried on the talk with, "In this presentation, we're going to discuss how we can avoid a similar fate and make sure we comply with the regulation."

INCLUDE A ROADMAP

Your presentation needs to provide your audience members with a Roadmap that shows exactly where they will be going and how they will be getting there. For example, during my public speaking seminars, I say:

> "During the workshop, you will first pick up three ways on how to create great content that keeps your audience wanting more. Next, you will discover three very specific formulas you can use to logically structure your speech for maximum impact. Finally, you will learn three delivery techniques you can use to bring your presentation alive for your audience!"

The above Roadmap lets my audience know that the workshop is split into three parts: Content, Structure and Delivery. What this does is create three mental folders in my audience's minds, one for each section of the seminar. Thus, audience members file the points for each section under the appropriate mental folders. This makes the presentation easier for audience members to follow and remember.

In his brilliant Commencement Address at Stanford University (AkashKaria.com/Steve), Steve Jobs gave a brief roadmap of his speech:

"I will be sharing with you three stories. That's all. Just three stories."

The lesson here is that you should include a short roadmap as part of your opening to let audience members know how your presentation is structured.

IN A NUTSHELL

- Do not open with a boring "me-focused" opening, a "thank you" or a joke
- Open with one or a combination of the following five gambits:
    - Story
    - Question
    - Quotation
    - Interesting/Startling statement
    - Callback
- Include a big promise (explicit or implicit)
- Use pain statements (explicit or implicit)
- Provide a roadmap

Spend plenty of time writing and re-writing your opening. Rehearse your opening. Get feedback regarding the start and ending of your speech from friends and colleagues. All the time you invest in perfecting the opening of your presentation will be worth it.

Chapter Five

BUILDING THE BODY OF YOUR PRESENTATION

The body of the speech is where you begin building the main points and arguments. Armed with your core message, you can build your argument logically and support your points using stories, statistics, analogies, activities, etc.

The key thing to keep in mind is that every time you make a point, you need to tie your point to an anchor.

What is an anchor?

An anchor is a device that you use to hook your point to your listeners' memories. You can use several types of anchors to support your main points.

10 ANCHORS TO MAKE YOUR POINTS MEMORABLE

Every time you make a point, you need to "tie it down" with an anchor. The mistake most presenters make is that they give too many points and don't use anchors to make their points stick. As a result, their points are forgotten.

You can choose any one of the following ten anchors to hook your points to your listeners' memory:

1. ANECDOTES (STORIES)

Tell a story that illustrates your main point. A well-told story acts like a memorable testimonial.

Now, for a second, imagine that you're a politician. Imagine that you're presented with the biggest opportunity of your life – the opportunity to speak at a large national convention, in front of thousands of people and millions more watching on TV. You're well known locally, but relatively unknown on the national stage. How would you begin that address?

In 2004, Barack Obama was selected to give the keynote address at the 2004 Democratic National Convention (DNC). At the time of the DNC keynote, Obama was an Illinois state senator, but he was relatively unknown on the national stage. The speech he gave turned him into a national star and led to talk about his potential for a future run for the presidency. Less than a minute into his speech at the DNC, Obama launched into a story that supports the main theme of his speech. Putting politics aside, the excerpt below of Obam's 2004 DNC speech (AkashKaria.com/Obama) is worth studying:

"Tonight is a particular honor for me because — let's face it — my presence on this stage is pretty unlikely. My father was a foreign student, born and raised in a small village in Kenya. He grew up herding goats, went to school in a tin-roof shack. His father — my grandfather — was a cook, a domestic servant to the British.

But my grandfather had larger dreams for his son. Through hard work and perseverance my father got a scholarship to study in a magical place, America, that shone as a beacon of freedom and opportunity to so many who had come before.

While studying here, my father met my mother. She was born in a town on the other side of the world, in Kansas. Her father worked on oil rigs and farms through most of the Depression. The day after Pearl Harbor my grandfather signed up for duty; joined Patton's army, marched across Europe.

Back home my grandmother raised a baby and went to work on a bomber assembly line. After the war, they studied on the GI Bill, bought a house through FHA and later moved west, all the way to Hawaii in search of opportunity.

And they, too, had big dreams for their daughter. A common dream, born of two continents.

My parents shared not only an improbable love, they shared an abiding faith in the possibilities of this nation. They would give me an African name, Barack, or "blessed," believing that in a tolerant America your name is no barrier to success. They imagined -- They imagined me going to the best schools in the land, even though they weren't rich, because in a generous America you don't have to be rich to achieve your potential.

They're both passed away now. And yet, I know that on this night they look down on me with great pride.

They stand here -- And I stand here today, grateful for the diversity of my heritage, aware that my parents' dreams live on in my two precious daughters. I stand here knowing that my story is part of the larger American story, that I owe a debt to all of those who came before me, and that, in no other country on earth, is my story even possible."

The story anchors the point that America is a great nation where hard work and perseverance pay off. I believe that a story is one of the best anchors you can use. It engages the emotional parts of people's brains and is one of my most reliable and consistently successful tools when giving a speech.

2. ACRONYMS

Here's a quick thought experiment. Imagine that you're in the military. You're part of the infantry scouts, which means that you're on the front line. You are in charge of the critical task of locating enemies and secretly reporting their activities. Having undergone military training, you have learned that you need to report the following items to Headquarters to provide the intelligence required to make an informed decision:

- SIZE - Approximately how many troops does the enemy have?
- LOCATION of enemy, using map-grid references.
- UNIT – What is the identity of the enemy?
- ACTIVITY – What sort of activities are being carried out by the enemy?
- EQUIPMENT – What equipment and weapons does the enemy have?
- TIME – Time and date of sighting.

Spend a couple of minutes memorizing the list above in the order provided.

Now, don't look back at the list. Imagine that you're on your first mission and you've spotted the enemy. Unfortunately, the enemy has spotted you too and you've been forced to engage in combat. The enemy opens fire on you – there's an exchange of bullets, screaming of orders, people hiding and ducking for cover, an explosion of rockets. You're dazed from the explosion of bombs. You have to write a quick report about the enemy's activities – to send intelligence back to Headquarters – but it's hard to think clearly. Under this situation, how well do you think you could remember the items required for reporting?

Granted, it's difficult to remember anything under those conditions. However, to make it easier for military personnel to remember the reporting requirements, the military has devised the S.A.L.U.T.E. acronym (**S**ituation, **A**ctivity, **L**ocation, **U**nit, **T**ime, **E**quipment). The SALUTE acronym takes the initial letter from each required reporting item and forms them into a word that troops can use to remember the items.

The military regularly uses acronyms to help its troops remember important concepts. For example, the acronym B.R.A.S.S. has been devised to help soldiers remember the techniques to shoot a gun accurately. BRASS stands for **B**reathe, **R**elax, **A**im, **S**lack and **S**queeze. Again, the acronym BRASS does a good job of helping soldiers remember the shooting instructions as opposed to a standard list of instructions.

The military isn't the only place where acronyms have been used to facilitate learning and recall. Students and teachers all over the world use acronyms to help students pass examinations. You might have used an acronym to help you remember important concepts for an exam.

If you have a list of points, experiment to see if you can perhaps create an acronym to help your audiences remember your points.

3. ACTIVITIES

If you can create some sort of quick game/role-playing activity that will solidify your point, then be sure to include it.

During my workshops, I use lots of activities to help participants internalize the concepts I am teaching. For example, I use an activity that teaches participants how stressing a particular word can change the meaning of an entire sentence. I get them to read out the following sentences with the stress placed on the word in italics and then ask them how that changes the meaning of the sentence:

- *I* didn't know she was upset
- I *didn't* know she was upset
- I didn't *know* she was upset
- I didn't know *she* was upset
- I didn't know she was *upset*

The point of the activity? What word you stress can completely change the meaning of the sentence.

If you are giving a workshop, seminar or presentation on creativity, you might split audience members into groups and give them an activity to find a creative solution to a problem you've given them.

An activity is a great anchor because:

- It gets your audience **physically moving and doing something.** If your audience members are physically moving and involved in *doing* something (as opposed to just sitting back and listening to you), you can be guaranteed that they're engaged ... and awake!

- It **reinforces your point.** An activity helps make your point memorable. They might forget what you said, but they won't forget what they did ... and when they remember the activity, they'll remember the point associated with it.

4. ANALOGIES, SIMILES, METAPHORS

One of the best ways to remember or learn something is to link the new topic you're trying to learn to something that you're already familiar with. In other words, the best way to learn is to create a bridge between the familiar and the unfamiliar.

Analogies, similes and metaphors compare two unlike objects to one another. They are great anchors because they take a subject that audience members are already familiar with and create a connection or a link between the known and the new information you're sharing.

For example, here's an example of an analogy from the book *The Mars and Venus Diet and Exercise Solution* by John Gray:

"Think of your body as an old-fashioned steam engine. You need to feed the fire with coal. When there is no coal available, the stoker slows down so that all the available fuel is not consumed.

Likewise, your metabolism slows down for the rest of the day when you don't eat breakfast."

5. STATISTICS

Statistics help make your points memorable. For example, the following statistic makes the point about wealth inequality very clear:

"Ninety-nine percent of the world's wealth is controlled by one percent of the world's population."

Here is another statistics that help make the points memorable because they provide evidence that the point is true.

"One bag of popcorn is as unhealthy as a whole day's worth of fatty foods!"

You'll pick up more tools on how to use statistics in your speech in Chapter 7 of this book.

6. ACADEMIC RESEARCH

Using academic studies to back up your point not only anchors your point, but also adds credibility to it. Research studies, if told well, are usually very fascinating because they arouse people's curiosity. Consider the following portion of Dan Pink's TED talk (AkashKaria.com/Dan) where he talks about Dan Ariely's research:

"Dan Ariely, one of the great economists of our time, he and three colleagues, did a study of some MIT students. They gave these MIT students a bunch of games, games that involved creativity, and motor skills, and concentration. And they offered them, for performance, three levels of rewards: small reward, medium reward, large reward. If you do really well you get the large reward, on down.

What happened?

As long as the task involved only mechanical skill bonuses worked as they would be expected: the higher the pay, the better the performance. Okay? But when the task called for even rudimentary cognitive skill, a larger reward led to poorer performance."

Research studies by nature try to answer questions. Thus, an explanation of the research study followed by the words "What happened?" raises the audience's curiosity.

If you are able to use an academic study in your speech to anchor your point, use it. Explain the study in the form of a story, and use rhetorical questions to build people's curiosity before you reveal the results.

7. CASE STUDIES
Case studies are another method to anchor your points.

For example, if you're giving a presentation called "Improving Brand Awareness through Social Media," you might give your audience members a case study of a company that embraced social media to increase its brand awareness. Then, you would work your way through the case study, highlighting the major points and providing insights on why the strategy worked and what could have been done better.

Using case studies is a very common way of teaching MBA classes. In fact, the Harvard Business School MBA course is taught using case studies.

8. PRODUCT DEMONSTRATIONS

If you're presenting or pitching a product, then a product demonstration is a brilliant way to win your audience's trust as well as make your points memorable.

The late Steve Jobs was a master at this. For example, during the unveiling of the Safari browser, Jobs wanted to make the point that Safari was much faster than Internet Explorer. Instead of simply saying this, Jobs gave a product demonstration. He launched both Safari and Internet Explorer on two separate big screens, typed in a web address and hit the button to load both pages at the same time. The result? Safari loaded the page within seconds while Internet Explorer was still fetching the data.

A memorable demonstration firmly ties the point to the audience's memories. Plus, it's tangible proof – no one can dispute the claim since they just witnessed the live demonstration.

If you're presenting or pitching a product, consider including a product demonstration as part of your presentation.

9. CUSTOMER TESTIMONIALS

If you're presenting to a prospective client with the hope of being hired, using customer testimonials is a great way to anchor your points and prove your worth.

For example, let's say you work for a company that produces computer chips for computer manufacturers. Now, let's say you're scheduled to give a presentation to a prospective computer manufacturer with the aim of getting their account. What might you include in a presentation such as this? What could you say that would persuade them to hire you?

If you're saying that your company produces widgets cheaper and faster than anyone else, then you might want to tell a story about a client who approached you because he needed computer chips produced very quickly, within a few days, because his last chip manufacturer had gone out of business. Next, you could showcase a testimonial by this client stating how pleased he was with your service. There are several ways to showcase the testimonial. You could include this testimonial in your PowerPoint or on your handout, or simply read the testimonial to your audience.

Since we are talking about testimonials, there are several things to keep in mind when using testimonials.

- **Video Testimonials are best**. Testimonials of clients speaking on video are the best because they are the most credible. Audiences trust video testimonials more than anything else because written testimonials are easy to fake. If you have a video testimonial, you can embed it as part of your PowerPoint presentation.

- **Use Photos of Clients.** If you can get hold of only a written testimonial, then try to include photos of your client. Including a photo as part of your testimonial gives it more credibility.

- **Include Names**. Include both the client's first and last names. Nameless testimonials are worthless because they lack credibility. They could easily have been faked. If you can, include where your client works and his/her position at the firm.

- **Use Testimonials that are specific.** While testimonials such as "Your company was great. I was thrilled with the service you provided!" are pleasing to receive, they are too general and vague to receive much credibility from your audience. Vague testimonials give very little detail about you or your company's specific benefits and strengths, which is why they're not valuable. Instead, consider asking your clients for specific testimonials such as: "Using your company's products helped me increase revenue by 45%. The product was easy to use and only took me one hour to learn. I anticipate that using your product will help me earn over $200,000 extra over the coming year."

10. QUOTES

Finally, you can use quotes to back up your main points and to make your message more memorable.

For example, during one of my speeches, I make the point that negative people can't affect you unless you let them. I then anchor my point with a quote. I say:

I realized that she wasn't the one making me feel inferior. I was the one making myself feel inferior because, like Eleanor

Roosevelt once said, "No one can make you feel inferior without your consent!"

A couple of months after I made my speech, I ran into a lady who'd been in my audience. She said, "I still remember what you told us. I remember your quote by Eleanor Roosevelt." To prove it to me, she proceeded to recite the quote for me.

In his TED talk, Sir Ken Robinson used a quote by Picasso to help support his main point that education kills creativity:

> Picasso once said this -- he said that "All children are born artists. The problem is to remain an artist as we grow up." I believe this passionately, that we don't grow into creativity, we grow out of it. Or rather, we get educated out if it. So why is this?

Quotes not only can be a great way to borrow credibility from a third-party source, they also can act as anchors that make your speech memorable.

IN A NUTSHELL

Use the following anchors to build the body of your presentation:
- Anecdotes
- Acronyms
- Analogies, Similes or Metaphors
- Activities
- Academic research
- Statistics
- Case studies
- Product demonstrations
- Customer testimonials
- Quotes

Chapter Six

CRAFTING A COMPELLING CONCLUSION

THE RECENCY EFFECT

Recency Effect: "Given a list of items to remember, we will tend to remember the last few things more than those things in the middle. We also tend to assume that items at the end of the list are of greater importance or significance" – <u>ChangingMinds.org</u>

Because of the recency effect, the ending of your speech is just as important as the beginning. People will remember the last thing that you say, so you want to make sure that you spend ample time crafting a great ending to your speech/presentation. Here are a couple of techniques that will help you craft a compelling and memorable closing.

SIGNAL THAT YOU'RE CLOSING

Studies show that when presenters use the words, "in conclusion," people become more alert. This is because the words "in conclusion" signal that the speech is coming to an end. Audience members know that the presenter will summarize the speech and that there may be some important follow-up tasks, so they start paying more attention to what's being said.

You don't necessarily have to use the phrase "in conclusion" to grab your audience's attention. You can use any other phrase to signal that you are coming to the end of your presentation. You can use phrases such as: "Let's wrap up," "To summarize" and "Before I leave the stage, let me leave you with this." Feel free to get creative with your closing signals as long as you make it obvious that you are closing.

SUMMARIZE YOUR MAIN POINTS

Use your closing to reemphasize your main points. The closing of your speech is your opportunity to call-back to your major points throughout the speech in order to reinforce them. The summary of your points should take, at most, two to three minutes. Here's an example from Dan Pink's TED Talk:

> "Let me wrap up. There is a mismatch between what science knows and what business does. And here is what science knows. One: Those 20th century rewards, those motivators we think are a natural part of business, do work, but only in a surprisingly narrow band of circumstances. Two: Those if-then rewards often destroy creativity. Three: The secret to high performance isn't rewards and punishments, but that unseen intrinsic drive -- the drive to do things for their own sake. The drive to do things cause they matter"

PROVIDE HOPE FOR A BETTER FUTURE

Not only should you summarize your main points, you also should provide hope for a better future. If you've presented a problem that needs to be conquered, you need to give your audience hope that it is possible to conquer it. End your speech on an uplifting note and leave your audience feeling empowered. To continue using our previous example, after Dan Pink summarized his main points, he ended his speech with the following:

> "And here's the best part. Here's the best part. We already know this. The science confirms what we know in our hearts. So, if we repair this mismatch between what science knows and what business does, if we bring our motivation, notions of motivation into the 21st century, if we get past this lazy, dangerous, ideology of carrots and sticks, we can strengthen our businesses, we can solve a lot of those candle problems, and maybe, maybe, maybe we can change the world. I rest my case."

Here's another example. Leslie Morgan Steiner ended her TED talk on domestic violence (AkashKaria.com/Leslie) by providing hope that they could solve the problem:

> "Recognize the early signs of violence and conscientiously intervene, deescalate it, show victims a safe way out. Together we can make our beds, our dinner tables and our families the safe and peaceful oases they should be. Thank you"

LINK YOUR CONCLUSION TO THE CONFERENCE

Sir Ken Robinson not only ended his speech by providing hope for a better future, he also linked his conclusion to the TED conference. He said:

"What TED celebrates is the gift of the human imagination. We have to be careful that we use this gift wisely and that we avert some of the scenarios we've talked about. And the only way we'll do it is by seeing our creative capacities for the richness they are and seeing our children for the hope that they are. And our task is to educate their whole being, so they can face the future. By the way - we may not see this future, but they will. And our job is to help them make something of it. Thank you very much."

Robinson not only manages to summarize the main arguments of his speech during his conclusion, he also manages to link it to the TED conference where he is speaking. This gives his speech a personalized feel and grabs audience attention.

During her TED talk, Dr. Jill Taylor (AkashKaria.com/Jill) also managed to end her speech by including TED's mission statement ("ideas worth spreading") in her closing. She said:

"I believe that the more time we spend choosing to run the deep inner-peace circuitry of our right hemispheres, the more peace we will project into the world, and the more peaceful our planet will be. And I thought that was an idea worth spreading."

If you can find a way to link your conclusion to the event where you are speaking, you will be miles ahead of most speakers. You can be assured that you'll have left a lasting impression on your audience.

INCLUDE A CALL TO ACTION
What do you want your audience members to do differently as a result of listening to your speech?

Include a clear and compelling call to action in the closing of your speech. Tell your audience members exactly what you want them to do. If you're presenting a business proposal to a group of senior managers and you want them to set up a second meeting with you, tell them:

> "As we've seen, this untapped market is worth $40 million every year. We've seen that the rewards far outweigh the costs and that the best time to start catering to this market is now. Having discussed this, I would like to request a second meeting so that we can discuss how to go forward from here."

What action do you want your audience to take after listening to your presentation?

Here are a couple of things to keep in mind when crafting your call to action:

- **Be realistic about what you can expect from them.** If you're pitching a business idea to a group of potential investors, then it's unrealistic to expect that they will invest a million dollars into your business immediately. Perhaps a more realistic call to action might be to ask them to set up a second meeting so you can talk about funding. Or you might ask them to invest in 10% of your company so that your company can get off the ground and they can monitor the progress before they decide to fully invest in you. In any case, make sure you have a realistic call to action.

- **Include only one call to action.** Don't paralyze your audience by giving them too many choices. Include only one clear and compelling call to action. For example, at the end of my workshops, instead of burdening my audience with a list of 20 things I want them to do, I just give them call to action, which is to head over to my website so that they can subscribe to my free newsletter. I can then keep in constant contact with them via my newsletter.

Normally, the first presentation is part of a series of more things to come, such as emails, meetings and presentations. For example, your sales presentation might lead to a second and third meeting before the client eventually buys from you. However, instead of burdening your prospects with a huge list of next steps, give them only one next step they can take so that you can lead them to the next phase of the process.

In her TED Talk on body language (AkashKaria.com/Amy), Amy Cuddy wraps up her speech by encouraging her audience to try power-posing. She also gives her audience a clear next step, which is to "spread the science":

"So I want to ask you first, you know, both to try power posing, and also I want to ask you to share the science, because this is simple. I don't have ego involved in this. (Laughter) Give it away. Share it with people, because the people who can use it the most are the ones with no resources and no technology and no status and no power. Give it to them because they can do it in private. They need their bodies, privacy and two minutes, and it can significantly change the outcomes of their life. Thank you."

What's the clear next step of your speech?

SELL THE BENEFITS

What benefits do audience members get as a result of acting on the wisdom received from your speech?

In his TED talk, Andy Puddicombe (AkashKaria.com/Andy) encourages audience members to practice 10 minutes of mindfulness. He ends his talk by reinforcing the benefits audience members will receive if they take just 10 minutes to focus on the present moment:

> "All you need to do is to take ten minutes out a day to step back, to familiarize yourself with the present moment so that you get to experience a greater sense of focus, calm and clarity in your life."

Consider closing your speech by summarizing the benefits your audience will get if they act on what they have learned in your speech.

IN A NUTSHELL

Close your talk with an impact by:

- Signaling you are closing
- Summarizing your main points
- Linking it to the conference
- Providing hope for a better future
- Providing a clear call to action
- Selling the benefits

PART 2:

UNEXPECTED

Boring presentations are predictable. On the other hand, an outstanding presenter stands out from the rest and grabs audience attention by doing or saying something unexpected. In this section, you will learn how to grab audience attention by doing something unexpected *without* being gimmicky:

More specifically, you will know how to add the element of "unexpectedness" by learning how to:

- Use shocking statistics and facts to grab audience attention
- Offer the audience something new (or unconventional)
- Create a WOW moment

Chapter Seven

USING STATISTICS TO GRAB ATTENTION

Using shocking statistics is a great way to capture audience attention. For example, look at how celebrity chef Jamie Oliver (AkashKaria.com/Jamie) used a startling statistic to grab audience attention in his 2010 TED talk:

> "Sadly, in the next eighteen minutes when I do our chat, four Americans that are alive will be dead from the food that they eat"

Wow, what a powerful and shocking statistic! One of the things that make this statistic very powerful is that Jamie puts the statistic into the audience's context. Instead of saying, "One hundred and seventeen thousand Americans die every year because of the food that they eat," Jamie makes the numbers easier to digest. A year is a very long time, so Jamie boils the statistic down to the same amount of time as the TED talk. Highlighting the number of deaths that take place during the TED talk makes the situation seem more urgent. It makes the audience members aware of the deaths taking place *right now* as they sit in the room.

Second, it's hard to digest 117,000 deaths ... at a certain point, if a statistic is too large, the sheer size of the figure causes audience members to become indifferent to the situation instead of causing empathy. However, four deaths is a smaller number to digest and imagine, so it causes audience members to become hopeful that it is a manageable situation.

Now, let's look at other ways you can use statistics in a speech.

If you were asked to write an article to convey to your readers the magnitude of Bill Gates' wealth in an interesting and memorable manner, how would you write it? Sure, you could quote Bill Gate's wealth of $40 billion from the Fortune website, but as you'll learn from the example of a Wall Street journalist, there's a much more effective way to make such statistics "sticky" by relating them to your listeners.

If you were called upon to make a speech to prove the fast pace of your company's technological innovation, what would you say? You could show colorful graphs that illustrate your company's total R&D expenditure and return on investment, but there's an even simpler technique you can pick up from Intel's CEO Paul Otellini.

If you were a leader whose task was to show a nation that the deficit had ballooned to dangerous levels, what would you say that would motivate people to call for a stop to the spending? You could unsuccessfully spout off various economic indicators, or you could do what President Dwight D. Eisenhower did to create a visual statistic that stuck in his listeners' minds.

However, before we examine the various ways that you can use statistics in your communication to create persuasive messages, we first need to address the issue of:

CREDIBILITY vs. MEMORABILITY

Look at the following two statistics:

(A) In the year 2009, more than 1,265,000 people died in China due to smoking.

(B) Approximately 2,000 people die each day in China due to smoking.

Statistics are a great way of adding credibility because they provide evidence for your point of view. In this case, both statements (A) and (B) provide credibility for your communication, although (A) provides more credibility because it gives the perception of accuracy. However, not many people will remember (A).

Statement (B), on the other hand, does a better job of "memorability." Your listeners are more likely to remember that "2,000 people die each day in China due to smoking" because it is a smaller number than (A) *and* it's rounded off.

So, if you want credibility, provide accurate statistics. (Just don't go crazy! One decimal point is enough for most cases.) If you want memorability, provide smaller numbers (e.g., instead of talking about the deaths per year, talk about deaths per day/hour/minute/second) and round the numbers off for easier recall.

However, there is a better solution. You could have **both** credibility *and* memorability with the following phrase:

> "In the year 2009, over 1,265,000 people died in China due to smoking. In other words, approximately 2,000 people a day died because of smoking."

In this sentence, we have both credibility from (A) and memorability from (B).

There is also another way to have both credibility and memorability, and that is with the use of fractions. Take the following two statistics:

(C) 66.7% of people in the U.K. have access to a computer
(D) 2 out of 3 people in the U.K. have access to a computer

In this example, (C) provides credibility, but (D) provides **both** credibility *and* memorability. Statement (D) is just the fraction form of (C) – it is still just as accurate, and it is easier to remember because small fractions are easier to remember than percentages.

Using statistics that are both credible and memorable helps make sure that your viewpoint will be both *accepted* and *remembered*. Now, let's look at how to make your statistics "sticky" by relating them to your listeners.

RELATE IT TO THE AUDIENCE

One way to make effective use of statistics is to relate them to your audience. Let's go back to the Bill Gates example. Here's how a writer for the *Wall Street Journal* related Gates' wealth to the average reader [I'll write it in my own words so that you can get the full gist of the technique being used]:

> "Let us say that you're an average person who earns an average salary. And let's say that one weekend you take your spouse to the cinema. Now, while you're standing in line you see that Bill and Melinda Gates are also paying for the same movie that you are going to be watching. The difference is: If Bill Gates was to pay the same percentage of his wealth that you pay, then it would cost him $19 million for the tickets alone!"

The reason that this statistic is effective is because it actively involves you: you are the comparison by which the statistic makes a point. Previously, you may have known that $40 billion was a lot of money, but it may have been very hard to put it into context. The strategy of "relating a statistic to the audience" puts scenarios in the context of the listeners' world – making the statistic more impactful and exciting.

Here's another example. In the movie *"Coach Carter,"* Coach Carter uses the following statistic:

> "In this county, thirty three percent of black males between eighteen and twenty four get arrested. So look at the guy on your left, now look at the guy on your right. One of you is going to get arrested."

Coach Carter relates the statistic in a powerful way that brings the reality home to his audience.

Relating your statistics to your audience turns boring statistics into powerful and memorable ones that grab and keep your audience's attention.

COMPARE AND CONTRAST

This technique is similar to the previous one in that it puts statistics in context of your listener's lives. However, while the last statistic directly involved your listener, this technique is similar to an analogy: it puts things in context by comparing them to other, more familiar environments.

For example, let's assume that you're a technophobe. You're bad at technology. However, due to your son's insistence, he's driven you down to see a talk by Intel CEO Paul Otellini. You didn't think you'd enjoy the talk, but thanks to Otellini's easy comparisons, you've managed to grasp just how quickly technology is changing. Here's how Otellini used the compare and contrast technique to relate technological innovation to something that's easier for you to understand – automobiles:

> "Today we have the industry's first-shipping 32-nanometer process technology. A 32-nanometer microprocessor is 5,000 times faster; its transistors are 100,000 times cheaper than the 4004 processor that we began with. With all respect to our friends in the auto industry, if their products had produced the same kind of innovation, cars today would go 470,000 miles per hour. They'd get 100,000 miles per gallon and they'd cost three cents."

While Otellini did use technology jargon and statistics ("microprocessor is 5,000 times faster"), he then compared the technological innovation of the nanometer microprocessor to that of the automobile. In this case, even though you didn't know much about microprocessors, you still managed to understand the main point of the statistic because it was put in context of something you do understand. Also, by comparing the development of the microprocessor to that of the auto industry, Otellini was able to come up with an exciting and shocking statistic (*"If their products had produced the same kind of innovation, cars today would go 470,000 miles per hour"*).

MAKE IT VISUAL

Is it possible to make a statistic visual?

In 1958, President Eisenhower wanted to convey to the public the true magnitude of the billion-dollar deficit. Like the Wall Street journalist who cleverly made Bill Gates' $40 billion more "real" by relating it to the audience, Eisenhower found a clever way to shock with a statistic by turning it into a visual. He said:

"To understand the billion-dollar deficit, imagine taking all the one-dollar bills in a billion and laying them out end to end. Why, it would more than go to the moon and back again!"

The visual of one-dollar bills going all the way to the moon and back again is startling. It's much more exciting and memorable than a statistic about a billion-dollar deficit.

IN A NUTSHELL

Use statistics to grab attention. The following techniques will give more impact to your statistics:

- Relate your statistic to your audience
- Compare and contrast
- Make it visual

Chapter Eight

OFFERING THE AUDIENCE SOMETHING NEW

The surest way to be boring is to be completely predictable. If your audience knows exactly what you're going to say, then why should they pay attention?

Earlier in the book, you learned two ways to avoid being predictable. First, avoid a predictable "Thank you for having me here" opening. Second, use startling statistics to make sure you don't lose your audience's attention. There are several other ways to make sure your presentation isn't completely predictable:

TALK ABOUT SOMETHING NEW

In his TED India talk, Pranav Mistry (AkashKaria.com/Pranav) got a standing ovation for his talk on the thrilling potential of SixthSense technology. He gave his audience a glimpse into the future by demonstrating how his SixthSense device would allow people to browse the Internet on any surface, create a telephone keypad on their palm and draw on any surface. The device is the stuff of sci-fi movies and will revolutionize the way we interact with the digital world. Because it was such an exciting and new topic, Pranav had the audience hooked into his talk right from the start.

Do you have something new and exciting to talk about? If not, don't worry! Lots of other speakers are in the same boat as you. The good news is that there are some other ways that you can avoid being completely predictable.

LOOK AT AN OLD TOPIC FROM A NEW PERSPECTIVE

If the topic you are going to be discussing has been overused, try putting a new spin on it or looking at it from a new perspective. For example, body language is a very common topic. Hundreds of thousands of talks are available on how to read other people's body language. In her TED talk, researcher Amy Cuddy approached body language from a new perspective (AkashKaria.com/Amy) – she talked about how our body language affects how we feel:

> "So when we think of nonverbals, we think of how we judge others, how they judge us and what the outcomes are. We tend to forget, though, the other audience that's influenced by our nonverbals, and that's ourselves"

ARGUE AGAINST CONVENTIONAL WISDOM

Thousands of talks are available on the Internet about the power of goal setting. It's conventional wisdom that goal setting helps you achieve more success. However, what if that's not true? What if, as some experts think, the best goal is no goal?

Arguing against conventional wisdom is a great way of keeping your audience hooked into your speech. Because you're taking an unexpected stand, your audience members will be interested in what you have to say and curious to find out why you are saying it. Of course, you should only argue against conventional wisdom if you think it's wrong.

Consider another example. It's conventional wisdom that more choices result in more happiness. The more choices you have about what to eat, the more satisfied you will be when you make your decision. The more choices you have about how to invest your money, the happier you will be. Right?

In his fascinating TED Talk, Barry Schwartz (AkashKaria.com/Barry) argues that having too many choices leads to the consumer feeling bewildered when making a choice and less satisfied even after choosing. His argument was backed up by research studies and examples. It was a very captivating TED talk because it changed the audience's view on the topic and gave them a new way to look at an old topic.

Now, you may be thinking, "Akash, what if I don't have anything new to talk about? What if I haven't invented anything revolutionary? What if the issue I want to address is something that lots of other speakers have already talked about before? What if I can't argue against conventional wisdom because the conventional wisdom is correct?" Again, don't worry. There are two other ways that you can avoid your presentation being entirely predictable.

DIG OUT STORIES FROM ACADEMIC RESEARCH

There are a lot of great stories hidden in academic research. However, most of these stories are known only within the academic circle. If you're willing to wade through the tomes of academic research, you can unearth great stories and statistics that you can use in your speeches and presentations to offer your audience something new.

Bestselling author Malcolm Gladwell is an expert at breathing life into academic research. My two favorite books by Gladwell, *"Blink"* and *"Tipping Point,"* bring to life stories from academic research.

In his TED talk on "Choice, Happiness and Spaghetti Sauce" (AkashKaria.com/Gladwell), Gladwell brings to life the story of Dr. Howard Moskowitz. This story was quite well known in the field of psychophysics, but wasn't well known to the general population. In his TED talk, Gladwell shares the story with his audience members. Here is a short excerpt from Gladwell's speech:

> "…I decided instead, I would talk about someone who I think has done as much to make Americans happy as perhaps anyone over the last 20 years. A man who is a great personal hero of mine. Someone by the name of Howard Moskowitz, who is most famous for reinventing spaghetti sauce.
>
> Howard's about this high, and he's round, and he's in his sixties, and he has big huge glasses and thinning grey hair, and he has a kind of wonderful exuberance and vitality, and he has a parrot, and he loves the opera, and he's a great aficionado of medieval history. And by profession, he's a psychophysicist. Now, I should

tell you that I have no idea what psychophysics is, although at some point in my life, I dated a girl for two years who was getting her doctorate in psychophysics. Which should tell you something about that relationship. (Laughter)

As far as I know, psychophysics is about measuring things. And Howard is very interested in measuring things. He graduated with his doctorate from Harvard, and he set up a little consulting shop in White Plains, New York. One of his first clients was -- this is many years ago, back in the early '70s -- one of his first clients was Pepsi. And Pepsi came to Howard and they said, "You know, there's this new thing called aspartame, and we would like to make Diet Pepsi. We'd like you to figure out how much aspartame we should put in each can of Diet Pepsi, in order to have the perfect drink." Right? Now that sounds like an incredibly straightforward question to answer, and that's what Howard thought. Because Pepsi told him, "Look, we're working with a band between eight and 12 percent. Anything below eight percent sweetness is not sweet enough, anything above 12 percent sweetness is too sweet. We want to know, what's the sweet spot between eight and 12?" Now, if I gave you this problem to do, you would all say, it's very simple. What we do, is you make up a big experimental batch of Pepsi, at every degree of sweetness -- eight percent, 8.1, 8.2, 8.3, all the way up to 12 -- and we try this out with thousands of people, and we plot the results on a curve, and we take the most popular concentration. Right? Really simple.

Howard does the experiment, and he gets the data back, and he plots it on a curve, and all of a sudden he realizes it's not a nice bell curve. In fact, the data doesn't make any sense. It's a mess. It's all over the place..."

INTERVIEW INTERESTING PEOPLE

You don't necessarily have to look through academic research to find great stories, although it is a good place to look for interesting stories which are relatively unknown to the general population. You can also tell interesting third-person stories about your friends, family and people who you've interviewed. For example, in his TED talk, Sir Ken Robinson shares the story of Gillian, a choreographer he interviewed for his book:

"...Anyway, Gillian and I had lunch one day and I said, "Gillian, how'd you get to be a dancer?" And she said it was interesting; when she was at school, she was really hopeless. And the school, in the '30s, wrote to her parents and said, "We think Gillian has a learning disorder." She couldn't concentrate; she was fidgeting. I think now they'd say she had ADHD. Wouldn't you? But this was the 1930s, and ADHD hadn't been invented at this point. It wasn't an available condition. (Laughter) People weren't aware they could have that.

Anyway, she went to see this specialist. So, this oak-paneled room, and she was there with her mother, and she was led and sat on this chair at the end, and she sat on her hands for 20 minutes while this man talked to her mother about all the problems Gillian was having at school. And at the end of it -- because she was disturbing people; her homework was always late; and so on, little kid of eight -- in the end, the doctor went and sat next to Gillian and said, "Gillian, I've listened to all these things that your mother's told me, and I need to speak to her privately." He said, "Wait here. We'll be back; we won't be very long," and they went and left her. But as they went out the room, he turned on the radio that was sitting on his desk.

And when they got out the room, he said to her mother, "Just stand and watch her." And the minute they left the room, she said, she was on her feet, moving to the music. And they watched for a few minutes and he turned to her mother and said, "Mrs. Lynne, Gillian isn't sick; she's a dancer. Take her to a dance school."

I said, "What happened?" She said, "She did. I can't tell you how wonderful it was. We walked in this room and it was full of people like me. People who couldn't sit still. People who had to move to think." Who had to move to think. They did ballet; they did tap; they did jazz; they did modern; they did contemporary. She was eventually auditioned for the Royal Ballet School; she became a soloist; she had a wonderful career at the Royal Ballet. She eventually graduated from the Royal Ballet School and founded her own company -- the Gillian Lynne Dance Company -- met Andrew Lloyd Weber. She's been responsible for some of the most successful musical theater productions in history; she's given pleasure to millions; and she's a multi-millionaire. Somebody else might have put her on medication and told her to calm down."

USE PERSONAL STORIES

Finally, personal stories are one of the best ways to breathe life into an old topic. Sharing your personal stories adds a new perspective into an old, worn-out topic. For example, in her TED talk on domestic violence, Leslie Morgan Steiner makes a potentially dull topic interesting and emotional by sharing her personal story:

"I was 22. I had just graduated from Harvard College. I had moved to New York City for my first job as a writer and editor at Seventeen magazine. I had my first apartment, my first little green American Express card, and I had a very big secret. My secret was that I had this gun loaded with hollow-point bullets pointed at my head by the man who I thought was my soul-mate, many, many times. The man who I loved more than anybody on Earth held a gun to my head and threatened to kill me more times than I can even remember."

IN A NUTSHELL

Avoid being predictable and boring by:

- Talking about something new
- Looking at an old topic from a new perspective
- Arguing against conventional wisdom
- Digging out stories from academic research
- Interviewing interesting people
- Using personal stories

Chapter Nine

CREATING A "WOW" MOMENT

If you want to be remembered, and if you want your audience to be talking about your presentations *months* after the actual presentation, you need to create a Wow-Moment. If you want to avoid your speech being completely predictable and boring, it helps to have a moment in your speech where your audiences' jaws drop in amazement.

In his TED talk, Pranav Mistry created a Wow-Moment by demo-ing his breakthrough sixth sense technology. By showing his audience how the virtual world could integrate with the real world, Pranav wow-ed his audience.

However, you don't necessarily have to demo breakthrough technology in order to wow your audiences.

For a perfect example of the Wow-Moment in a business presentation, let's examine Steve Jobs' presentation at Macworld 2008 (AkashKaria.com/Mac). During the presentation, Jobs said that the MacBook was "so thin it even fits inside one of those envelopes you see floating around the office." Jobs then pulled the new MacBook Air out of a manila office envelope just to show everyone how thin it was. The audience roared with applause and laughed with delight. That moment became the most talked-about moment of the event – bloggers blogged about it, journalists wrote about it and fans raved about it. It was also the most common photograph of the conference. They say that a picture is worth a thousand words; this dramatic demo was worth a thousand pictures.

Let's look at another example of a Wow-Moment, this time from a TED conference where Dr. Jill Taylor brings out *an actual brain* for illustration purposes:

> "If you've ever seen a human brain, it's obvious that the two hemispheres are completely separate from each other. And I have brought for you a real human brain. So this is a real human brain"

You can hear the audience gasp when they realize it's an actual brain! The blogosphere was buzzing with excitement about Dr. Taylor's Wow-Moment, which is how I originally stumbled across the talk.

What can you do to wow your audiences? Perhaps you can show a demo? Or use a prop to make your idea more concrete?

What's your wow factor?

IN A NUTSHELL

Avoid being predictable and boring:

- Create a wow-moment
- Demo a remarkable product or use a prop to make your idea more concrete
- Do something which will get your audience buzzing with excitement

PART 3:

CONCRETE

The best presentations are concrete rather than vague. They provide specifics and paint clear images in the audience's minds. They try to turn abstract concepts into concrete ideas.

In this section, you will learn how to make your messages concrete by learning how to:

- Use specific, concrete language
- Bringing your characters to life by providing specific details
- Turning your stories into mental movies for your audience using the VAKS formula
- Use analogies, metaphors and examples to turn abstract ideas into images

Chapter Ten

BE SPECIFIC

There once was a shepherd boy who was bored as he sat on the hillside watching the village sheep. To amuse himself he took a great breath and sang out, "Wolf! Wolf! The Wolf is chasing the sheep!"

The villagers came running up the hill to help the boy drive the wolf away. But when they arrived at the top of the hill, they found no wolf. The boy laughed at the sight of their angry faces.

"Don't cry 'wolf', shepherd boy," said the villagers, "when there's no wolf!" They went grumbling back down the hill.

Later, the boy sang out again, "Wolf! Wolf! The wolf is chasing the sheep!" To his naughty delight, he watched the villagers run up the hill to help him drive the wolf away.

When the villagers saw no wolf they sternly said, "Save your frightened song for when there is really something wrong! Don't cry 'wolf' when there is NO wolf!"

But the boy just grinned and watched them go grumbling down the hill once more.

Later, he saw a REAL wolf prowling about his flock. Alarmed, he leaped to his feet and sang out as loudly as he could, "Wolf! Wolf!"

But the villagers thought he was trying to fool them again, and so they didn't come.

At sunset, everyone wondered why the shepherd boy hadn't returned to the village with their sheep. They went up the hill to find the boy. They found him weeping.

"There really was a wolf here! The flock has scattered! I cried out, "Wolf!" Why didn't you come?"

An old man tried to comfort the boy as they walked back to the village.

"We'll help you look for the lost sheep in the morning," he said, putting his arm around the youth, "Nobody believes a liar...even when he is telling the truth!"

The fable above, "The Boy Who Cried Wolf," was written by Aesop. Aesop's fables are some of the stickiest stories ever written. Some of Aesop's other sticky stories you may have heard are "The Tortoise and the Hare," "The Fox and the Grapes" and "The Goose that Laid the Golden Eggs." Written more than 2,500 years ago, these fables have survived the test of time.
So what makes them so sticky?

What can we learn from them about creating sticky presentations?

One thing that makes Aesop's fables sticky is that they are concrete – they provide images that make the ideas come alive in your mind. For example, you can *see* the boy in your mind, you can *hear* him shout and you can *feel* his happiness at having tricked the villagers. The story is rich in sensory information, which makes it concrete. It provides specific details and paints vivid pictures in your mind's eye. These details make the story memorable.

This brings us to our first tip for creating concrete presentations: provide specific details. Use specific language that paints vivid images in your listeners' minds. Specificity aids memory. Abstract concepts are forgotten. Concrete ideas that provide specific details are remembered. In your presentations and speeches, provide specific details. For example, instead of saying, "A couple of years ago …" say "Three years ago ..." or "In 2010 …".

In her TED talk, Dr. Jill Bolte Taylor embraces the principle of specificity by saying:

> "But on the morning of December 10, 1996, I woke up to discover that I had a brain disorder of my own."

Do you notice how much more powerful that is than saying, "But one morning a couple of years ago, I woke up to discover I had a brain disorder of my own"?

Similarly, instead of saying, "I was living in a wonderful hotel," say "I was living in Room 201 of the Ritz-Carlton Hotel in Palm Beach." Do you see how providing the specific details makes the description come alive? Do you notice how saying "Ritz-Carlton Hotel in Palm Beach" creates a completely different atmosphere than saying "a wonderful hotel"? Also, this description paints a very specific and vivid image of the Ritz-Carlton in Palm Beach –

it packs in a lot of sensory information, making it memorable for your audience.

To make your presentations and speeches memorable, give specific details and paint images in your audiences' minds.

IN A NUTSHELL

Avoid being predictable and boring by:

- Abstract concepts are easily forgotten
- The secret to stickiness is specificity
- Make your descriptions specific and vivid

Chapter Eleven

BRINGING YOUR CHARACTERS TO LIFE

Great speeches aren't just *heard;* they're also *experienced* in the audience's heads. Executive speech coach Patricia Fripp says, "People don't remember what you say as much as they remember what they see when you say it." If you want your audience to remember and *experience* your speech, you should paint mental images in their heads.

In his TED talk, Malcom Gladwell brings to life the character of Howard by providing lots of specific detail about him:

> "Howard's about this high, and he's round, and he's in his 60s. He has big huge glasses and thinning grey hair, and he has a kind of wonderful exuberance and vitality. He has a parrot, and he loves the opera, and he's a great aficionado of medieval history. By profession, he's a psychophysicist."

One of the things that make Gladwell such a superb storyteller is the fact that he knows how to breathe life into his characters. He does this by providing his audience with just enough sensory information to be able to picture the characters in their heads.

Another thing to learn from Gladwell is the way he follows the principle of showing rather than telling. He says that Howard "has a parrot, and he loves the opera, and he's a great aficionado of medieval history." This information gives you a hint about Howard's personality – it shows you his quirkiness rather than simply telling you about it.

Similarly, if a character in your speech is an alcoholic, instead of simply saying that "John had an alcohol problem," you should *show* this by saying "Every day after work, John would come back home and pop open a bottle of beer. He would sit at his table, alone, downing one bottle after another, until finally, around midnight, dozens of empty beer bottles later, he would fall asleep slumped over the table."

In your speeches and presentations, provide specific, sensory details about your characters to make them come alive in your audience's minds. Follow the principle of showing rather than telling.

IN A NUTSHELL

- Bring your characters alive by providing details about their appearance
- Give your audience enough sensory information to construct a mental image of your main characters
- Show, don't tell

Chapter Twelve

TURNING YOUR STORIES INTO MENTAL MOVIES

Mike Rowe is the host of the series *"Dirty Jobs"* on Discovery Channel. In his speech on "Learning from dirty jobs" (AkashKaria.com/Mike) Rowe talks about a job where he has to castrate sheep. Examine the following portion of his speech:

> "In the space of about two seconds, Albert had the knife between the cartilage of the tail, right next to the butt of the lamb, and very quickly the tail was gone and in the bucket that I was holding. A second later, with a big thumb and a well calloused forefinger, he had the scrotum firmly in his grasp. And he pulled it toward him, like so, and he took the knife and he put it on the tip. Now you think you know what's coming, Michael -- you don't, OK? He snips it, throws the tip over his shoulder, and then grabs the scrotum and pushes it upward, and then his head dips down, obscuring my view, but what I hear is a slurping sound, and a noise that sounds like Velcro being yanked off a sticky wall..."

Did you feel grossed out by the description?

Did you perhaps scrunch up your face in disgust, as I did when I heard that portion of the speech?

Did that scene play out mentally in your head like a movie?

Why did that scene affect you so powerfully?

The reason that the scene affects you so much is because it contains a lot of sensory information that brings the scene alive in your mind. Because it contains so many vivid details, you can't help but watch the scene playing out in your head.

The secret to turning your stories into mental movies for your audience is to make sure your scene is rich in sensory inputs. There are four senses that you need to cover: Visual, Auditory, Kinesthetic and Smell (VAKS).

Let's examine each of the VAKS in Rowe's speech:

Visual - what could you *see* in the story? You could see the knife and you could see the man firmly holding the sheep's scrotum with his "big thumb and well-calloused forefinger."

Auditory - what could you *hear?* You could hear the slurping sound, "like Velcro being yanked off a sticky wall."

Kinesthetic - what could you *feel?* You could probably feel Albert *firmly* holding the scrotum in hand. You might even have been able to feel the sheep's pain (even though that isn't specifically mentioned in the scene).

Smell - what could you smell? In this particular scene, there is no input for smell. However, smell is a powerful sense for transporting your audience into your scene.

If you want to turn your stories into mental movies for your audience, make sure you cover the VAKS. As this example shows, you don't have to give details about all four sensory inputs, but it is recommended that you do cover at least three out of the four VAKS in order to fully transport your audience into your story.

Also, as this example shows, the descriptions of your scenes don't need to be very long. You're telling a story, not writing a novel! In fact, the shorter your descriptions, the faster your story will move along and the more impactful it will be.

IN A NUTSHELL

Turn your scenes into mental movies using the VAKS:

- Visual - what could you see?
- Auditory - what could you hear?
- Kinesthetic - what could you feel?
- Smell - what could you smell?
- Pack in as many of the senses as possible
- Keep your descriptions short

Chapter Thirteen

USING ANALOGIES, METAPHORS AND SIMILIES

In his TED talk, Andy Puddicombe (AkashKaria.com/Andy), a monk, used juggling as an analogy for practicing mindfulness. While juggling three orange balls, he said:

> "So for example, right now, if I focus too much on the balls, then there's no way that I can relax and talk to you at the same time. Equally, if I relax too much talking to you, then there's no way I can focus on the balls. I'm going to drop them. Now in life, and in meditation, there'll be times when the focus becomes a little bit too intense, and life starts to feel a bit like this..."

Analogies build a bridge between two concepts or ideas. An analogy demonstrates how two things are alike by pointing out shared characteristics. In his analogy, Andy Puddicombe equates thinking with juggling.

An analogy is a powerful tool for making your ideas concrete. It can be used to aid understanding by comparing an unknown idea or subject to one that is more familiar.

Metaphors and similes are similar to analogies. A metaphor is a figure of speech that uses one thing to mean another and makes a comparison between the two. Here's an example of a metaphor by Shakespeare:

"All the world's a stage"

While an analogy compares the characteristics of two things and builds a logical argument based on that, a metaphor says that one thing *is* another. Here is another example of a metaphor by author Wayne Dyer:

"Your body is a garage to park your soul"

A simile is a comparison that links two different things by using the word "as" or "like."

In his *I Have a Dream* speech, Martin Luther King used the following simile:

"until justice rolls down like waters and righteousness like a mighty stream …"

In his TED talk, Andy Puddicombe also uses similes to make his speech more concrete. He says:

"You know, the mind whizzes away like a washing machine going round and round, lots of difficult, confusing emotions, and we don't really know how to deal with that, and the sad fact is that we are so distracted that we're no longer present in the world in which we live."

The second simile he uses compares meditation to aspirin:

"I assumed that it was just like an aspirin for the mind. You get stressed, you do some meditation."

You don't really need to memorize the differences among analogies, similes and metaphors in order to be able to use them effectively. Just know that comparing two different things and likening them to each other is a powerful public speaking tool.

To come up with your own similes, metaphors and analogies, ask yourself, "What can this idea be compared to? What are its main characteristics and how are they similar to other concepts?"

IN A NUTSHELL

- Use analogies, similes and metaphors to make your speech more concrete and memorable.
- Ask yourself, "What can this idea be compared to?"
- Try different analogies and metaphors until you find one which works best for your speech

PART 4:

CREDIBLE

In this section, you will learn how to make your messages credible by learning how to:

- Build your credibility during your introduction
- Add internal credibility to your messages

Chapter Fourteen

BUILDING CREDIBILITY WITH YOUR INTRODUCTION

We've all heard that "first impressions are important," but what you may not realize is that first impressions are *everything!* People's first impressions of us are extremely crucial because everything we do afterwards gets filtered through their initial impressions of us.

In other words, if someone initially thought you were selfish, then everything else you do afterwards (say, you pay for their meal) will be interpreted as selfish. ("He paid for my meal. He probably wants a favor from me.")

Perhaps a study by Harold Kelley (1950) will prove just how important initial impressions are. In this study, students were informed that a guest lecturer was coming to the university. Some of the students were given Description A [below] about the lecturer and the others were given Description B:

A. Cold person, industrious, critical, practical and determined

B. Warm person, industrious, critical, practical and determined

As you can see from the list, all the words on the list are identical – except for the first one. How would this affect the students' perceptions of the lecturer?

As it turns out, the students who read Description A had a harsher perception of the lecturer than those who read Description B – even though all the words other than the first ones were the same. What's even more surprising is that those who had been told that the guest lecturer was "cold" gave him much lower ratings than those who had been told he was "warm."

What does this have to do with public speaking?

A bad introduction can spell disaster for your speech even before you begin speaking. A great introduction, however, can enhance your credibility as a speaker and get your audience excited and fired up about listening to you.

Since a great introduction is so crucial to the success of a speech, it is your responsibility to make sure that your introducer gives you an introduction that will set you up for success. I generally recommend that you write your own introduction and give it to the person introducing you. Simply send them an email saying, "To make your job easier, I've got an introduction that you might like to use. I've attached it to this email for you to look through."

If, for some reason, it isn't possible to get your written introduction to the person who will be recommending you, I suggest you chat with him/her before the event to make sure that you are okay with his/her introduction.

Here are four principles you should follow when writing your own introductions (or introducing someone else):

SHARE RELEVANT CREDENTIALS

Academic degrees, awards and appearances in the media are symbols of authority. These symbols are credibility badges for speakers. A speaker who has a PhD, appeared on CNN, wrote for Fortune magazine and won the Nobel Prize is going to have a ton of credibility. The thinking is that, "If this speaker has a PhD, it means that he's knowledgeable. Plus, if CNN trusts him and I trust CNN, then it obviously follows that I should trust him."

When writing your introduction, consider the following questions: Why are you qualified to speak on this topic? Do you have a degree in it? Have you published a book or a paper on it? Have you won any awards for your work in this field? Have you written for any well-known publications? Have you appeared on any TV or radio shows?

One important and obvious point is that you should only share your *relevant* achievements. Sure, you may have won an award for being the fastest swimmer in school, but if your speech is about how to retire as a millionaire, it obviously follows that you should not include that achievement in your introduction (unless, of course, your swimming award somehow relates to being a millionaire).

You may be thinking, "Of course I know to include only my relevant achievements!" but you may be surprised at how many people violate this obvious guideline. Sometimes speakers are so attached to the awards they won in the past, they feel that they *have* to include them in the introduction (even though the awards have nothing to do with the topic at hand). Don't make the same mistake!

SHARE YOUR STRUGGLES BEFORE YOUR SUCCESSES

You don't have to have a PhD and appear on CNN in order to gain credibility as a speaker. In fact, some of the best motivational speakers in the world promote the fact that they *don't* have degrees. For example, the popular motivational speakers Les Brown and Anthony Robbins openly share with their audiences the fact that they don't have any formal education beyond high school. So, how are these speakers able to win the trust of their audiences?

The answer lies in the fact that the speakers share their struggles as well their successes. An introduction to a Les Brown seminar usually begins with the story of Les Brown's struggle, and then goes on to share the story of Les Brown's success. Let's have a look at a typical introduction of Les Brown:

> "Les Brown is a popular motivational speaker, author and coach who helps people have a larger vision for their lives. Les Brown's life itself is a testament to the infinite human potential. Born in an abandoned building on a floor in Liberty City, a low-income section of Miami, Florida, Les was adopted at six weeks of age by Mrs. Mamie Brown, a 38 year old single woman who had very little education or financial means.
>
> In the fifth grade, Les Brown was mistakenly declared "educably mentally retarded" and placed back in the fourth grade and later

failed the eighth grade. The label and stigma severely damaged his self-esteem for many years. Mamie Brown's believe in her son's ability to achieve whatever he set his mind to achieving made a difference in his life.

Les Brown's determination and persistence searching for ways to help Mamie Brown overcome poverty and his philosophy "do whatever it takes to achieve success" led him to become a distinguished authority on harnessing human potential and success. Les Brown's passion to learn and his hunger to realize greatness in himself and others helped him to achieve greatness in spite of not having formal education or training beyond high school."

By sharing your struggles in your introduction, you let your audience know that you are just like them – that you have gone through the same struggles they may be going through. It gives the audience the feeling, "If he can do it, so can I!" This helps you create empathy and build a connection with your audience.

Next, when you share your story of success, you win the respect of your audience for having overcome your struggles. You also gain credibility because you managed to turn your struggles into successes. To paraphrase Anthony Robbins, "You may not have a PhD, but you do have a PhD in results!"

When sharing your success, try to share as many specifics as possible. If you are giving a talk on weight loss and you lost weight, how much weight exactly did you lose? If you went from being in debt to being a millionaire, exactly how much debt were you in and how many millions do you have now? People associate specificity with credibility, so make sure you share the specifics!

USE PAST CLIENT TESTIMONIALS

A third way to gain credibility as a speaker is to use client testimonials in your introduction. For example, let's say Melissa is a consultant who's giving a speech about best consulting practices. Part of her introduction could include an excerpt from a testimonial she received from her work with Microsoft:

> As a consultant, Melissa has worked with 400 of the Fortune 500 companies. Bill Gates' said, "Melissa is one of the best independent consultant's Microsoft has hired. We expect her marketing strategy will increase our profits by $200 million this year." In this presentation, Melissa will share with you her five tips for becoming a highly-paid and sought after consultant…

ANSWER THE WIIFM QUESTION

One of the most important parts of the introduction is to answer the audience's "What's in it for me?" question.

Apart from building your credibility as a speaker, your introduction also has to fire up your audience for your presentation. It has to get them excited about what's coming next.

Therefore, in your introduction, you need to make it clear what benefits your audience will receive from your speech. After establishing the speaker's credibility, the introduction should tell the audience what value they will get from the speech. Thus, continuing with the previous example, this part would look something like this:

> "In this presentation, Melissa will share with you her five tips for becoming a highly-paid and sought after consultant. By the end of the presentation, you will have learned the exact process she used to land a six-figure contract with Microsoft. You will walk

away with the exact marketing blueprint she uses every time to get big clients knocking on her door instead of chasing after them. You will also pick up a special technique Melissa uses to get an additional $20,000 in income every time she lands a consulting assignment. So, if you're ready to become a highly-paid and sought-after consultant, please welcome Melissa..."

IN A NUTSHELL

Provide the emcee with your written introduction. Make sure your introduction follows the following guidelines:

- Share relevant credentials to establish yourself as an expert
- Share your struggles before your successes
- Use past client testimonials
- Answer your audience's WIIFM question

Chapter Fifteen

ADDING INTERNAL CREDIBILITY TO YOUR MESSAEGES

If you want to tell compelling stories that will leave your audience no choice but to be caught up in them, then you must use this next technique. It is a psychological technique so influential that it can unconsciously sway your judgments even when you are required to be objective. To understand this psychological technique, we have to head over to the University of Michigan.

Imagine that you are a part of the following experiment, which was carried out in 1986 by two researchers at the University of Michigan, Jonathan Shedler and Melvin Manis. In this experiment, you are assigned the role of a juror deciding whether Mrs. Johnson is capable of continuing to care for her seven-year-old son. You are given a case to read, with eight arguments for and eight arguments against Mrs. Johnson. You are required to analyze the arguments, and then come to an objective conclusion by indicating on a scale of 1-10 (10 being highest) how well you think Mrs. Johnson can take care of her son.

Okay, got that? Great!

Now think of a friend - a friend who you believe is an objective and rational person like you. Let's involve your friend in this experiment too. Your friend also is assigned the role of juror and told that his job is to be as objective as possible while analyzing the eight arguments for and against Mrs. Johnson.

Now, if the two cases are exactly the same, we can expect that both of you will come to a fairly similar conclusion.

However, imagine that you received Case A and your friend received Case B. Each case contains eight arguments for and eight arguments against Mrs. Johnson. However, for the sake of space and time, the cases below contain just one argument for and one argument against Mrs. Johnson. See whether you can spot the difference between Case A and Case B, and try to predict whether this minor difference is enough to affect your judgment (on the next page):

	CASE A	CASE B
FOR Mrs. Johnson	Mrs. Johnson sees to it that her child washes and brushes his teeth before bedtime. He uses a "Star Wars" toothbrush that looks like Darth Vader.	Mrs. Johnson sees to it that her child washes and brushes his teeth before bedtime.
AGAINST Mrs. Johnson	The child was sent to school with a badly scraped arm, which Mrs. Johnson had not cleaned or attended to. The school nurse had to clean the scrape.	The child was sent to school with a badly scraped arm, which Mrs. Johnson had not cleaned or attended to. The school nurse had to clean the scrape. As the nurse was cleaning the scrape, she spilled Mercurochrome on herself, staining her uniform red.

Did you manage to pick out the subtle differences between Case A and Case B?

In case you missed it, Case A contains the vivid, easy to picture image of the "Star Wars" toothbrush whereas Case B doesn't. Similarly, Case B contains the vivid image of the nurse spilling the

Mercurochrome and "staining her uniform red" whereas Case A doesn't.

The experiment is set up so that for Case A, all the eight favorable arguments for Mrs. Johnson contain vivid details that are easy to picture; for Case B, all the eight unfavorable arguments against Mrs. Johnson contain vivid details such as the spilling and staining of the uniform.

However, none of these vivid details should make a difference to the logic and reasoning of the case. They are both irrelevant to the question of whether or not Mrs. Johnson was a good mother.

So, are these irrelevant but vivid details enough to sway you and your friend's judgments about Mrs. Johnson? It turns out that even though these irrelevant details should not have mattered, they did.

The researchers found that those people who read Case A (with the vivid details included in the arguments for Mrs. Johnson) were more likely to judge Mrs. Johnson as a good mother than those people who read Case B (with the vivid details included in the arguments against Mrs. Johnson). In fact, those who read Case A rated Mrs. Johnson, on average, a 5.8 in terms of suitability as a mother, whereas those who read Case B rated her 4.3 (out of 10).

This seems strange, doesn't it? Why should the irrelevant detail of the "Star Wars" toothbrush in Case A make a person think Mrs. Johnson is a better mother than does someone who read Case B (without that detail of the "Star Wars" toothbrush)? While it matters that Mrs. Johnson makes sure her child brushes his teeth every night, it certainly doesn't matter that he uses a "Star Wars" toothbrush!

However, as the results from the research show, the vivid details did make a significant difference in the ratings of Mrs. Johnson. But how can this be?

The reason is that providing vivid details gives the message internal credibility. Because the "Star Wars" toothbrush makes it easy for jurors to picture the child brushing, they unconsciously perceive it to be more credible.

Let us have a look at another example of adding internal credibility to a speech by providing specific details. Take a look at the following two descriptions:

1. "You know, a while back, I met a man who told me that he was heading to Iraq soon."

2. "You know, a while back, I met a young man named Seamus in a VFW hall in East Moline, Illinois. He was a good-looking kid, 6'2", 6'3", clear eyed, with an easy smile. He told me he'd joined the Marines and was heading to Iraq the following week."

The second line is from Obama's 2008 Democratic National Convention speech. Obama realizes that vivid details are more memorable than vague statements. Just like the "Stars Wars" toothbrush and the spilling and staining red of the nurse's uniform, Obama's description creates a specific picture in your mind and engages you visually. It involves your imagination in creating the picture of a man who is 6'2" with an easy smile, and as a result, it's memorable. It also seems more credible than the first statement simply because it contains a lot more details.

The principle at play here is that specific details are more memorable *and* credible than vague statements. For example, instead of saying, "He was well-dressed," say, "He was dressed in a black, crisp Brooks Brothers suit." Not only will your message be more visually appealing, it will also be more memorable and be perceived as being more credible.

IN A NUTSHELL

Build internal credibility into your speech by providing specific and vivid details about characters and events.

PART 5:

EMOTIONAL

In this section, you will learn how to make your messages emotional by learning how to:

- Build the we-connection
- Address the elephant in the room
- Unite people towards a common enemy
- Highlight the pain before offering a solution
- Use compelling visuals to arouse audience's emotions
- Arouse curiosity - tease before you tell
- Use humor to engage the audience's emotions
- Use rhetorical questions to get the audience to reflect on their own lives

Chapter Sixteen

BUILDING AN EMOTIONAL CONNECTION WITH YOUR AUDIENCE

Malcolm X's "The Ballot or the Bullet" speech (AkashKaria.com/MalcolmX) was one of the greatest speeches ever delivered.

Whether or not you agree with the message, you can pick up a few tips on public speaking, speechwriting and persuasion from it.

In this chapter, we will analyze Malcolm X's speech to see what lessons we can learn from it about building an emotional connection with our audience:

ADDRESS THE ELEPHANT IN THE ROOM

The first step in building an emotional connection with your audience is to address any problematic issues up front. By addressing the elephant in the room at the beginning of your speech, you ensure that there are no barriers preventing you from connecting with your audience.

For example, in his "Ballot or Bullet" speech, Malcolm X immediately addresses the main issue concerning his religion. He knows that people are going to have questions about his faith, so he addresses those questions straight away by saying:

> "Before we try and explain what is meant by the ballot or the bullet, I would like to clarify something concerning myself. I'm still a Muslim; my religion is still Islam. That's my personal belief…Although I'm still a Muslim, I'm not here tonight to discuss my religion. I'm not here to try and change your religion."

In your speeches and presentations, if there are any problematic issues that your audience members are going to be thinking about, then address them straight away. Unless you first address the problematic issue ("the elephant in the room"), your audience members won't pay full attention to your speech because they will be thinking, "Yeah, but what about this other issue that you haven't addressed?"

Dispel people's fears and doubts by dealing first with the elephant in the room.

UNITE PEOPLE TOWARDS A COMMON GOAL

After addressing the issue of faith, Malcolm X builds an emotional connection with his audience by uniting them towards a common goal. He lets them know that they are all on the same team, working towards the same goal:

"I'm not here to argue or discuss anything that we differ about, because it's time for us to submerge our differences and realize that it is best for us to first see that we have the same problem, a common problem, a problem that will make you catch hell whether you're a Baptist, or a Methodist, or a Muslim, or a nationalist. Whether you're educated or illiterate, whether you live on the boulevard or in the alley, you're going to catch hell just like I am. We're all in the same boat..."

When giving your speech or presentation, make sure you unite people towards a common goal. Let everyone know that you're working towards the same goal.

UNITE PEOPLE BY FOCUSING ON A COMMON ENEMY

Nothing unites people more than fighting a common enemy. In his "Ballot or Bullet" speech, Malcolm X unites his audience members (mostly a group of African Americans) by pointing out the common enemy. He says:

"We're all in the same boat and we all are going to catch the same hell from the same man. He just happens to be a white man. All of us have suffered here, in this country, political oppression at the hands of the white man, economic exploitation at the hands of the white man, and social degradation at the hands of the white man."

Malcolm X then details who this enemy is and how he oppresses and exploits African Americans. This gets the entire crowd worked up to fight together against the common enemy. It builds a strong emotional connection with the audience by tapping into their primal instincts for self-defense.

In your speeches and presentations, look to see if you can unite your audience members by focusing on a common enemy.

For example, in a business presentation, your common enemy might be your competitor. The common enemy could be high costs. Any common enemy, along with a common goal, will win you your audience's support.

HIGLIGHT THE PROBLEM AND BUILD THEIR PAIN

Before you offer a solution, build up people's pain. Highlight all the pain that people are experiencing before you offer a solution. The more pain your audience feels, the more enthusiastic they will be about the solution.

In his speech, before offering his "solution," Malcolm X highlights the problem that the people in his audience are experiencing (note: "The Man" refers to the white man who oppresses blacks):

> "And because these Negroes, who have been mislead, misguided, are breaking their necks to take their money and spend it with The Man, The Man is becoming richer and richer, and you're becoming poorer and poorer. And then what happens? The community in which you live becomes a slum. It becomes a ghetto. The conditions become run down."

Highlighting the problem and building up people's pain makes them desperate to find your solution.

In your speeches and presentations, always highlight the problem first (and then build on the pain) before you offer a solution.

BUILD THE "WE-CONNECTION"

In his speech, Malcolm X lets his audience members know that he is one of them. He is a part of their community. He lets them know that he is facing the same problems and challenges that they are. He does this by using the "We-Connection":

> "So we're trapped, trapped, double-trapped, triple-trapped. Anywhere we go we find that we're trapped."

The We-Connection lets your audience members know that you are a part of their group. It lets them know that you are on their side because you are facing the same challenges that they are.

If you want to gain your audience's trust and support, then in your next presentation or speech build the We-Connection.

IN A NUTSHELL

Build an emotional connection with your audience by:

- Addressing the elephant in the room
- Uniting people towards a common goal
- Uniting people by focusing on a common enemy
- Highlighting the problem and building their pain
- Building the we-connection

Chapter Seventeen

USING COMPELLING VISUALS

Visuals can be a powerful way of arousing people's emotions. If you will be using a PowerPoint presentation, avoid filling your slides with boring, dry text – instead, fill your slides with large, visually stunning images that arouse strong emotions in your audience.

For example, if you are telling a story about rape victims in India, you might consider including a picture of a rape victim who has clearly been beaten and hurt. The pain in her eyes, the tears on her cheeks and the expression on her face will arouse strong emotions in your audience. That picture will affect people in a way that your words simply cannot.

Pictures are also a great way to increase the memorability of a presentation. According to research, three days after a presentation, most people only remember 10% of what they heard. However, if you add a picture, recall shoots up to 65%.

However, before you dive into creating your own PowerPoint presentation, ask yourself, "Is a PowerPoint really necessary?" Is the PowerPoint really going to aid your audiences' understanding of the message or are you simply using it as a crutch to remember what you have to say next? The only reason to use PowerPoint is if you have a lot of visuals – pictures, photos, charts and graphs you need to display. For example, in his TED talk, when describing an experiment, Dan Pink displayed an image that showed the experiment set-up:

> "Suppose I'm the experimenter. I bring you into a room. I give you a candle, some thumbtacks and some matches. And I say to you, "Your job is to attach the candle to the wall so the wax doesn't drip onto the table." Now what would you do?" [PowerPoint shows picture of candle, thumbtacks and a box of matches on a table next to the wall]

In this case, the visual aids the understanding of the message because seeing the experiment set-up makes it clearer how it works.

Similarly, in her TED talk about escaping poverty (AkashKaria.com/Jacqueline), Jacqueline Novogratz displays photos of a slum she visited in Kenya. The photos make the situation much more real for the audience and help them understand the poverty in Kenya because they can see proof of it.

If you do indeed determine that using PowerPoint will increase the effectiveness of your presentation, here are some guidelines to keep in mind when designing your slides:

1. LARGE PICTURES

One of the mistakes many presenters make is that they fill up their PowerPoint slides with too much text and too many bullets. They end up creating slideuments — a cross between a Word document and a Powerpoint presentation.

Having a lot of text on a slide quickly tires your audience's eyes and sends them to sleep. Furthermore, if your slides contain a lot of text, it's very difficult for even experienced presenters to avoid reading the text word for word. Finally, if your PowerPoint makes complete sense without you having to explain it, you're not needed … you might as well email your PowerPoint to your audience and cancel the presentation. As speech coach Craig Valentine puts it, "If you and your PowerPoint are saying the same exact thing, one of you is not needed."

The solution to this is to have no text or a minimum amount of text on your slides. Instead, fill up your slides with large, visually stunning images that complement what you are saying. For example, if you are talking about the impact of global warming, have a large picture that *shows* a glacier melting. This is much more powerful than having a slide filled with bullet points about melting glaciers.

No matter what your presentation is about, it's possible to turn it into a powerful visual which helps solidify your content. For an example of how to turn almost any concept into a visual, check out this PowerPoint presentation on Slideshare that walks you through the entire process (AkashKaria.com/Slideshare).

2. LARGE FONTS

If you do need to have some text on the screen – perhaps a quote or some keywords – make sure you use large fonts. Design your presentation for the person sitting at the back of the room. I advise that the text size of your font should be at least 30 points. This ensures that everyone in the room will be able to read the text and forces you to limit the amount of text on your slides.

3. ONE IDEA PER SLIDE

Don't overwhelm your audience with too many ideas on one slide. Use as many slides as you need, but stick to the rule of one idea per slide. This will keep your slides clutter-free. For example, if we go back to your presentation on the impact of global warming, instead of listing all the consequences of global warming on one bullet-filled slide, have a slide for each consequence and display a visually stunning photo, chart or image that shows the consequence.

This is by no means an exhaustive list of how to use PowerPoint effectively, but I believe that following the above three guidelines will ensure that you avoid many of the mistakes most presenters make when using PowerPoint. I realize that it would be helpful for you to have samples of effective PowerPoint slides, so I have created this Slideshare presentation that features some of the best PowerPoint slides I have seen (AkashKaria.com/PowerPoint) I have seen. I think you'll find it helpful. You can also check out my book on "How to Design TED-Worthy Presentation Slides" at AkashKaria.com/TEDWorthy.

IN A NUTSHELL

- Use a PowerPoint presentation only if you have lots of visuals to display
- If you and your PowerPoint are saying the same thing, one of you is not needed
- Use large, visually stunning pictures
- Use large fonts
- Only one idea per slide

Chapter Eighteen

AROUSING THEIR CURIOSITY

This tool has been used to influence you countless times – *and you may not even realize it!* It's been used to keep you up late at night. It's been used to influence your choices about what to watch. It's been used to keep you glued to your TV screen.

Have you ever found yourself stuck between doing some work and watching a TV show? "I'll just watch it till they cut to the commercials, and then I'll get started working," you tell yourself.

If you happened to be watching Larry King's "*25th Anniversary Special*," then this is what you would have heard Larry King say right before they cut to commercials:

> "Bette Davis, Bill Cosby, the Beatles, Sinatra. You don't want to miss this. It's all coming up on LARRY KING LIVE 25."

You don't want to miss it because the next segment sounds exciting. So you keep watching – and watching …

Oprah, Ellen and Larry King all use tantalizing teasers to keep you hooked to their shows. A tantalizing teaser is a sentence or two that tells you how great the next segment of the show will be, and as a result, you keep coming back after the commercial breaks.

Here are a couple of tantalizing teasers you may have heard on TV shows:

"After the break, find out how this woman lost over 200 pounds in two months. Stay tuned and she'll teach you her foolproof system to losing weight without a sweat!"

"Coming up next we have a man who has spent over 25 years researching the science of happy relationships. He interviewed over two thousand couples, consulted with religious leaders and read through tomes of academic literature on happiness. When we come back, he'll show you the three most important things you must do if you want to have a happy marriage. And no, they're not what you think!"

In their book, "*Made to Stick,*" Dan and Chip Heath give a great example of an online video called "The Girl Effect" (AkashKaria.com/Girl) which does a great job of teasing the audience into wanting to know more. The video starts by recounting a list of global problems: AIDS. Hunger. Poverty. War. It then teases you with the following question, "What if there was an unexpected solution to this mess? Would you even know it if you saw it? The solution isn't the Internet. It's not science. It's not government."

See, aren't you curious to find out the answer?

Two elements make the tantalizing teaser for "The Girl Effect" so effective. First, it makes great use of questions. The human mind has no choice but to start thinking about potential answers to a question. Second, it challenges you by letting you know what it's *not:* "It's not science. It's not government." These are solutions that most people would immediately jump to when hearing the questions, so by eliminating those choices, "The Girl Effect" video keeps you intrigued to find out what the correct answer is.

Tantalizing teasers are also used in presentations. Take this example from Darren LaCroix (AkashKaria.com/Darren), the 2001 Toastmasters International World Champion of Public Speaking, who used a tantalizing teaser during a workshop on presentation skills:

> "For my preparation for the World Championship, I was studying 10 years worth of contest videos. For those of you not familiar with the contest, it starts out with 25,000 contestants and comes down to just 9…and they videotape it every year. I got hold of those video tapes. I watched 10 years of contest videos: 90 world class speeches! I watched every one of them, and then I created a video-tape of just the winners, and I watched it over and over again, because I wanted to see "What was the tiny little difference between the person that came in first and the person who came in second?" At this point, Darren takes a long pause, and then continues, "And I have found four things that they have in common that you can do in your very next presentation…"

See, aren't you just dying to know what those four things are? Darren has *teased* you into listening to the rest of his speech.

In his TED talk, Simon Sinek also uses a tantalizing teaser before giving away his discovery. He teases:

> "About three and a half years ago I made a discovery. And this

discovery profoundly changed my view of how I thought the world worked, and it even profoundly changed the way in which I operate in it. As it turns out, there's a pattern. As it turns out, all great and inspiring leaders and organizations in the world - whether it's Apple or Martin Luther King or the Wright brothers - they all think, act and communicate the exact same way. And it's the complete opposite of everyone else. All I did was codify it, and it's probably the world's simplest idea..."

If you haven't watched Simon's talk (AkashKaria.com/Simon), I bet you're curious to find out what Simon's discovery is. I know I was!

The main job of the tantalizing teaser is to serve as an attention-grabbing transition between your points by conveying the importance of the message that's going to be given next.

The tantalizing teaser primes your audience to listen. If you want your audience to become excited and curious about what you have to say, tease them first before you tell them!

There are two places you can use tantalizing teasers in your presentation. First, if you are giving a workshop or a seminar, you can use a tantalizing teaser right before the break to keep your audience excited about the coming segment.

Second, you could also use a tantalizing teaser right before making a point. For example, let's say that you are giving a presentation on three ways to be more productive. Average presenters would remove all the mystery from their presentation by beginning with, "There are three ways to be more productive. First, wake up early. Second, set goals. Finally, go to bed before midnight. Let's start with the first one ..." This is by no means a *terrible* presentation. At least it has a clear structure. However, it isn't a good presentation either. It becomes completely predictable and boring because there's no curiosity factor left. This is one of the reasons why I recommend that presenters shouldn't show all their bullet points at once because there's no curiosity left about what's coming next. Instead, if you have bullet points on your slide, use animations to reveal each bullet point as you talk about it.

So, how would a good speaker approach a presentation? First, she would not reveal all her solutions at once. Second, she would tease before revealing her information. For example, for the presentation above, the speaker would say something along the lines of:

> "In this presentation, you will pick up three keys you can use to lead a more productive lifestyle. The first key will not only help you achieve twice as much in half the time, it'll also make you feel happier and energetic. Just imagine, how much more could you achieve if you could be twice as productive? I picked up this first key when..."

The speaker teases the audience by offering the benefits of the information before she offers the point. She also asks a rhetorical question to get the audience to reflect on how they would benefit if the presentation did make them twice as productive. Finally, instead of revealing the information immediately, she dives into an engaging story so that the audience can discover the answer within the story.

Here's another great example of a tantalizing teaser by researcher Brene Brown during her TED talk on "The power of vulnerability" (AkashKaria.com/Brown) she teased:

> "But here's what I can tell you that it boils down to - and this

may be one of the most important things that I've ever learned in the decade of doing research..."

See, you're burning to know what she learned, aren't you?

In your presentations and speeches, keep your audience curious by teasing before you tell. Use tantalizing teasers before breaks and before revealing important points.

IN A NUTSHELL

- Don't take your audience's curiosity for granted
- Tease before you reveal an important point or information
- Tease about what's coming up in the next segment before any breaks in your presentation

Chapter Nineteen

HOW TO ADD HUMOR TO YOUR TALK

Humor is a great way to engage your audience in your speech. Not only does humor keep your audience interested in your presentation, it also aids learning. Some of the most popular and inspiring TED talks of all time are also the most humorous. For example, in Sir Ken Robinson's popular TED talk, he makes the audience laugh an average of once a minute. Dan Pink's TED talk also contains great humor.

We've already discussed in earlier chapters that you should avoid jokes. So, how can you add humor to a presentation without resorting to telling jokes?

CREATE AN EXPECTATION, THEN SUDDENLY BREAK IT

A comment is humorous when it creates an expectation and then suddenly breaks it. We laugh when we are surprised. This is why we usually burst into laughter when we see someone suddenly trip and fall on their face. It was unexpected – it was a surprise – and it causes us to laugh. The side benefit of laughter is that it makes us more alert, which aids learning.

Ken Robinson is a master at creating expectations and then breaking them. Consider the following line:

> "If my wife is cooking a meal at home, which is not often... thankfully." (audience laughs)

In comedy, the part of the line that creates the expectation is called the set-up. In this case, the set-up is "If my wife is cooking a meal at home, which is not often ..." Sir Ken's set-up makes us think that he is complaining about his wife not cooking often enough. The punch line refers to the part of the line that suddenly breaks the expectation. In this case, the punch line is the word "thankfully." It suddenly breaks our earlier expectation because we find out Sir Ken is actually *glad* his wife doesn't cook often!

The thing that makes a comment humorous is the *sudden* breaking of the expectation. Thus the shorter the punch line, the greater the laugh. If Sir Ken had said, "If my wife is cooking a meal at home, which is not often, and I'm thankful about that," the comment wouldn't have been as funny. If you want to produce a gigantic laugh from your audience, keep your set-up and punch line as short as possible.

Here's another example of this technique from Dan Pink's TED talk:

> "I didn't do very well. I, in fact, graduated in the part of my law school class that made the top 90 percent ... possible." (audience laughs)

The set-up creates the expectation that Dan graduated at the top of his class. The punch line of "possible" suddenly breaks that expectation and gives us new insight that Dan graduated in the bottom of his class. Our brain realizes that it's had a verbal trick performed on it, and so we laugh. The other reason this line works so well because it's self-deprecating humor – Dan is poking fun at himself.

USE SELF-DEPRECATING HUMOR

Self-deprecating humor refers to making yourself the butt of the jokes. If you're willing to make fun of yourself, you'll never run out of humorous possibilities.

Consider the following piece of self-deprecating humor from Dan Pink's TED talk:

> "I never practiced law a day in my life; I pretty much wasn't allowed to." (audience laughs)

Self-deprecating humor works because it shows that you're willing to poke fun at yourself. It gives the audience permission to have fun because you're having fun by making fun of yourself. Furthermore, it makes you more likeable as a speaker because we all like people who take themselves lightly.

Here's another piece of self-deprecating humor from Sir Ken Robinson's TED talk:

> "I used to be on the board of the Royal Ballet in England ... as you can see."

Sir Ken pokes fun at himself. It's obvious from looking at him that he doesn't do ballet.

The lesson here is this: don't be afraid to poke fun at yourself on stage.

OVER-EXAGERRATE

People also laugh at obvious over-exaggerations. Consider the following piece of humor from Elizabeth Gilbert's TED talk (AkashKaria.com/Gilbert):

> When I first started telling people -- when I was a teenager -- that I wanted to be a writer, I was met with this same kind of, sort of fear-based reaction. People would say, "Aren't you afraid you're never going to have any success? Aren't you afraid the humiliation of rejection will kill you? Aren't you afraid that you're going to work your whole life at this craft and nothing's ever going to come of it and you're going to die on a scrap heap of broken dreams with your mouth filled with bitter ash of failure?" (audience laughter)

The obvious over-exaggeration of the last comment is what causes people to laugh.

In his TED talk, Sir Ken also used over-exaggeration to get a laugh from his audience. Consider how grossly he over-exaggerates his wife's ability to multi-task:

> "If she's cooking, you know, she's dealing with people on the phone, she's talking to the kids, she's painting the ceiling, she's doing open-heart surgery over here" (audience laughter)

Here's another example of over-exaggeration from the same talk by Sir Ken:

> [If you are at a party and someone asks] "What do you do?" and you say you work in education, you can see the blood run from their face. They're like, "Oh my God," you know, "Why me? My one night out all week!" (audience laughter)

There are entire books devoted to humor, but I find that the above three techniques are the ones from which I generate the bulk of laughs.

IN A NUTSHELL

Use the following techniques to add humor to your presentation:

- Create an expectation, then suddenly break it
- Poke fun at yourself using self-deprecating humor
- Playfully over-exaggeration to get a laugh from your audience

Chapter Twenty

USING RHETORICAL QUESTIONS

Asking rhetorical questions is a great way to get your audience emotionally engaged in your speech. Rhetorical questions give audience members the opportunity to reflect on their lives, thus helping to build an emotional connection between your speech and their lives.

RHETORICAL QUESTIONS THAT ASK YOUR AUDIENCE TO IMAGINE

For example, if you were giving a speech on the power of focus, you could ask the question, "Just imagine: how would your life be different if you had the ability to focus 100% on what needed to be done? How much more would you be able to achieve? What goals would you finally be able to achieve?"

This rhetorical question gets audience members to imagine their lives being better if they could do whatever it is that the speech promises to help them do. It gets the audience members excited about the speech because they are excited about improving their lives.

Notice that the rhetorical question is much more powerful than the statement, "If you had the ability to focus 100% on what needed to be done, you would be able to achieve so much more in life!" The rhetorical question invokes an emotional response from the audience by getting them to imagine their lives, whereas the statement simply goes in one ear and out the other.

RHETORICAL QUESTIONS THAT ASK YOUR AUDIENCE TO REFLECT

You can also use rhetorical questions to get your audience to reflect on their lives. For example, in a speech I once gave about my ex-girlfriend (whom I called Nancy Negative), I told a story about Nancy Negative shooting down my dream with her negativity. I then asked the audience, "Who is your Nancy Negative?" This rhetorical question took an object out of my speech (in this case, Nancy Negative) and put it into the audience's lives. This rhetorical question got the audience to reflect on all the negative people who were killing their hopes and dreams.

Similarly, if you are telling a story about mountain climbing, you could ask your audience the following rhetorical questions: "What mountain are you climbing? What peak are you trying to reach?" Such questions take an object out of your speech (in this case, the mountain or peak) and put it into the audience's lives. It gets the audience to reflect on their lives, the obstacles they are facing and the goals they are trying to achieve in their lives.

Rhetorical questions don't necessarily have to get the audience to reflect on their lives. They can also get the audience to reflect on their society. For example, if you are giving a speech on gun violence, you might say: "Every day, two hundred children die in acts of gun violence. How many more have to die before we take action?" This question invokes powerful emotions in the audience because it gets them to reflect on the state of their society and, at the same time, makes them feel responsible by implying that they have the ability to prevent the deaths.

RHETORICAL QUESTIONS THAT REFLECT YOUR AUDIENCE'S THOUGHTS

Rhetorical questions can also be used to voice out loud your audience's thoughts. If you voice your audience's thoughts aloud, your audience members will feel connected to you. They'll think, "Wow! That's exactly what I was thinking."

For example, in her TED talk on body language, Amy Cuddy knew that her audience would be wondering about the practical applications of the theory she had shared with them. Therefore, she asked the following rhetorical questions:

> "But the next question, of course, is can power posing for a few minutes really change your life in meaningful ways? ... Where can you actually apply this?"

Similarly, if you know your audience members will be thinking, "What happened to Mr. ABC after he made decision XYZ?", you can simply say, "You're probably wondering, 'What happened to ...?'" This builds a rapport with your audience, helps move your story along and creates curiosity about what happened next.

To make the best use of this tool, go through one of your speeches (either the transcript of your speech or an audio/video recording of it). As you listen to your speech, put yourself into your audience's shoes and ask yourself, "As an audience member, what questions pop into my mind?" Use this knowledge to voice out loud what your audience might be thinking in the form of rhetorical questions.

RHETORICAL QUESTIONS THAT ASK YOUR AUDIENCE TO COMPARE

Finally, rhetorical questions can also get the audience members to compare between two choices.

The most famous question of this type comes from Ronald Reagan, who said during the 1980 presidential election:

> Ask yourself, "Are you better off now than you were four years ago? Is it easier for you to go and buy things in the stores than it was four years ago? Is there more or less unemployment in the country than there was four years ago? Is America as respected throughout the world as it was?"

Notice how this question stirs more powerful emotions in the audience than simply saying, "We were better off four years ago than we are today." The question asks the audience to reflect on their life at present, compare it with four years ago and come to the inevitable conclusion that they aren't better off. Since it's the audience members who come to that conclusion, they are more likely to buy into the argument than if they had that conclusion thrust on them by Reagan.

Here's another comparison question from Zig Ziglar:

"Are you a wandering generality or a meaningful specific?"

This rhetorical question gets audience members to reflect on their lives to find which one they are, and they naturally make the conclusion that they want to be a meaningful specific.

Rhetorical questions are very powerful in arousing audience emotions. Use rhetorical questions to get your audience to imagine, reflect and compare, and to voice out loud your audience's questions.

IN A NUTSHELL

Use rhetorical questions to arouse your audience's curiosity and keep them emotionally engaged in your presentation. There are several types of rhetorical questions. Rhetorical questions that:

- Ask your audience to imagine
- Ask your audience to reflect
- Reflect your audience's thoughts
- Ask your audience to compare

PART 6:

STORY

In this section, you will learn how to make your messages stick using stories. We've already discussed a lot about storytelling – you have learned that your stories should be rich in sensory details (VAKS), that you should describe your characters and that you should be specific when describing scenes. Since we've already covered those concepts, we won't cover them again here. Instead, we'll examine some new storytelling tools you can use to tell exciting stories that keep your audiences hooked.

More specifically, you will learn the:

- Importance of storytelling
- 5C's of great stories
- Delivery techniques for dynamic storytelling

Chapter Twenty-One

HOW SUBWAY USED A STORY TO INCREASE SALES BY TWENTY PERCENT

Did you hear about the guy who lost more than 200 pounds in less than a year? And that he did this by eating only fast food?

In November 1999, an article that appeared in *Men's Health* featured a bizarre story about Jared Fogle. According to the article, Fogle was an overweight student at Indiana University who managed to lose 245 pounds on his "Subway diet" — a diet that consisted of him eating only Subway sandwiches.

When the management at Subway heard about this, they decided to scrap their "7 under 6" campaign (a series of ads that promoted the fact that Subway had 7 sandwiches with under 6 grams of fat) and to market Jared's story instead.

The result? As soon as "Jared the Subway guy" commercials began running, sales jumped by almost 20%. However, after a few years of Jared's commercials, Subway began to remove Jared from their ads. With Jared gone, sales began to go down. So Subway decided to bring Jared back and sales shot back up again.

Why is it that Jared's story was such a huge hit? Why was the Jared-story more successful than the "7 under 6" campaign?

The answer lies in the fact that stories are much more persuasive than statistics. Or, as executive speech coach Patricia Fripp puts it, "People are trained to resist a sales pitch, but no one can resist a good story." It's easy to resist the "7 Under 6" campaign, but Jared's story is so inspiring that we cannot help but watch it. We get involved in Jared's story – as humans, we empathize with his problem of being overweight, even though we may not be overweight ourselves. We get involved in the story because we are curious ("Wow! How did he lose so much weight?"), and we get involved because we can "see" the story – that is, even if you haven't watched the Jared commercials, you can still mentally picture a "before-Subway" and "after-Subway" Jared.

The "7 Under 6" campaign, on the other hand, is a statistic which informs us, but fails to involve us because it doesn't inspire us. It doesn't make us curious. We can't even picture what six grams of fat would mean for our body.

As we've seen, stories are a powerful form of communication. They're engaging because they involve us emotionally, and they are memorable because we can mentally see the story. To be successful in our communication, we must use stories.

IN A NUTSHELL

Stories are powerful because they:

- Engage your audience emotionally
- Create mental movies in your audience's mind
- Make abstract ideas visual

Chapter Twenty-Two

FIVE C'S OF GREAT STORIES

The essence of public speaking is to tell a story and make a point.

But what exactly makes a great story?

What are the elements that go into creating stories that captivate your audience members?

What kind of stories should you include in your speeches and presentations?

In this chapter, you will learn the five C's of great stories. We'll look at how Jared's Subway story fits within the 5C's framework. We'll also examine Leslie Morgan Steiner's story to see how Leslie used the 5C's to deliver a captivating story. I suggest that you first watch Leslie's speech on surviving domestic violence before you read further: AkashKaria.com/Leslie.

1. YOUR STORIES MUST HAVE CHARACTERS

Who are the main characters in your story?

Give a hint about what your main characters look like so audience members can visualize the characters. Provide a little bit of information about the characters' appearances so that audience members can "see" the characters.

Let's take the Subway story as an example. Who's the main character? Jared Fogle.

What basic information have we been given about him? He is an overweight student at Indiana University. Even though you're reading this, the information you've been given is enough for you to construct a mental picture of Jared.

What about Leslie's speech? The two characters in Leslie's speech are Leslie and her ex-husband. Since Leslie is standing on stage, we don't need any description of her. What about her ex-husband? What information do we have about him? Leslie tells us that her ex-husband, Conor, "had just graduated from an Ivy League school, and that he worked at a very impressive Wall Street bank ... he was smart and funny and he looked like a farm boy. He had these big cheeks, these big apple cheeks and this wheat-blond hair, and he seemed so sweet." Leslie gives us enough information about Conor to create a mental image of him in our heads.

When telling stories in your speeches and presentations, make sure that you provide some specific details about how your main characters look.

2. YOUR STORY MUST HAVE A CONFLICT

The conflict is the hook of the story. The conflict is what keeps audience members curious to find out what happens next in the story. Your audience members become interested in finding out how the conflict will be resolved.

For example, what was the main conflict in the movie *"Titanic"*? The ship was sinking and people were struggling to stay alive. More specifically, the two main characters – Jack and Rose – were struggling to stay alive. Would they stay alive? Would they die? There was also a secondary conflict in the movie regarding Jack and Rose's relationship. Would they find a way to be together? Or would they break up because they were from such different backgrounds?

Every great movie you watch or great book you read has a main conflict that keeps you hooked to find out how (or whether) the conflict will be resolved.

Again, let's take Jared's story as an example. What's the conflict? The conflict at the beginning of the story is that Jared is struggling to lose weight. He's overweight and out of shape and life seems to be going nowhere for him, but he wants to change that.

What's the conflict in Leslie's story?

"Conor used my anger as an excuse to put both of his hands around my neck and to squeeze so tightly that I could not breathe or scream, and he used the chokehold to hit my head repeatedly against the wall. Five days later, the ten bruises on my neck had just faded, and I put on my mother's wedding dress, and I married him. Despite what happened, I was sure we were going to live happily ever after, because I loved him, and he loved me so very much....It was an isolated incident, and he was never going to hurt me again.

It happened twice more on the honeymoon. The first time..."

The conflict in Leslie's story is that she is being physically abused by her then-husband but can't leave him because she's in love with him and keeps believing he will change.

3. YOUR STORY MUST HAVE A CURE

The conflict needs to be resolved in some way.

What's the cure that resolves the conflict?

The cure should help audience members overcome the conflicts they may be facing in their own lives. The cure is what adds value to your audience's life.

In Jared's story, the cure comes in the form of the Subway diet. The Subway diet helps Jared overcome his battle against obesity and lose 245 pounds.

What's the cure in Leslie's story?

"I was able to leave, because of one final, sadistic beating that broke through my denial. I realized that the man who I loved so much was going to kill me if I let him. So I broke the silence. I told everyone: the police, my neighbors, my friends and family, total strangers..."

The cure is that Leslie finds the courage to leave Conor because of one final beating which broke through her denial.

4. CHARACTERS MUST CHANGE AS A RESULT OF THE CONFLICT

What personality/attitude shifts do your characters undergo as a result of having overcome the conflict?

How do they see the world differently as a result of having been through the conflict?

How do they change physically, emotionally or spiritually because of the conflict?

For example, after going through hardship, a character may become tougher. After struggling through poverty, a character may start up a business and become wealthy (rags to riches story).

For Jared, he goes from being extremely overweight to being in decent shape. He goes from feeling horrible to looking and feeling better because of his Subway sandwich "cure."

In Leslie's story, the change is that she goes from being in an abusive relationship to finally getting out of it. She goes from being in denial about her situation to finally accepting that the man she loved so much was going to kill her. Furthermore, she goes from keeping her abusive relationship a secret to sharing her story with the world so that she can help others in similar situations.

5. YOUR STORY MUST HAVE A CARRYOUT MESSAGE

The essence of public speaking is to "tell a story and make a point."

So, what's the point of your story?

What's the one thing you want your audience members to remember from your story/speech/presentation? This is your Carryout Message that audience members will take home with them. It's the key takeaway message for your audience.

The Carryout Message of the Subway story is that Subway sandwiches are a healthy choice! After all, they allowed Jared to lose 245 pounds.

What's the Carryout Message of Leslie's story? Leslie uses her story to take us through the different steps of a domestic violence relationship, but the final Carryout Message for her audience is that instead of blaming victims of violent relationships for staying in those relationships, we should "recast survivors as wonderful, loveable people with full futures. Recognize the early signs of violence and conscientiously intervene, de-escalate it, show victims a safe way out."

After having examined Jared's Subway story and Leslie's personal story, we can see that the 5C's structure makes up the foundation for effective stories. Apply the 5C's to create stories that keep your audiences hooked onto your every word.

IN A NUTSHELL

Captivate your audience with stories. Make sure your stories contain the five essential C's of storytelling:

- Characters
- Conflict
- Cure
- Change in character
- Carryout message

Chapter Twenty-Three

DELIVERY TECHNIQUES FOR DYNAMIC STORYTELLING

It's not enough to have a great story. You also need to know how to deliver it in a way that keeps your audiences on the edge of their seats. While it's difficult to learn delivery techniques from a book, you can still learn some important delivery devices which will make you a dynamic speaker:

PAUSE BEFORE YOU BEGIN

Most speakers make the mistake of getting up on stage and beginning to speak immediately. Instead, I recommend that you get up on stage and make eye contact with your audience for a couple of seconds before you even say your first word. This is a way of acknowledging your audience and building a connection with them before you begin speaking.

Pausing at the beginning has several other advantages. First, it shows that you're a confident speaker who's not afraid of silence.

Second, it allows everyone in the room to get on the same vibration and energy level. For example, let's say that your audience members are chatting among themselves when you get up on stage. By pausing for a couple of seconds, you give your audience members time to stop their conversations and focus their attention on you. Finally, pausing at the beginning of your speech allows you to gain confidence. If you're nervous about speaking, use the pause at the beginning of your speech to take in a couple of subtle yet deep belly-breaths to calm yourself down. I usually get nervous before an important presentation, but by pausing for a couple of seconds before I start, I can usually get rid of the butterflies in my stomach.

SMILE

When you get on stage, you should generally smile at your audience to show that you acknowledge their presence. However, don't try to fake a smile, because studies show that people are subconsciously able to detect a fake smile. Get yourself into a mindset where you truly value your time with the audience. Realize that you have been given a wonderful opportunity to share your message with the world. Getting yourself into this positive mindset will help you smile.

The only time you should not smile when you get up on stage is if you want to create tension in the room. For example, if you are about to deliver a sad story that begins with the death of a loved one, it would not be appropriate to start off with a smile.

Generally, though, I recommend smiling at your audience. A smile reveals your warmth and your sincerity and is the first step in establishing an emotional connection with your audience.

MAKE EYE CONTACT

Making eye contact with your audience is a great way to gain their trust. We associate eye contact with sincerity and lack of it with lying. Thus, make eye contact with your audience members as often as possible.

I recommend the scan and stop method for making eye contact. When you are delivering your story, scan the room with your eyes so that you briefly make eye contact with people in each section of the room (front, back, left, right and center). However, when you come to an important point, stop and look one person in the eye and deliver your point directly to them. Similarly, when you ask an important question, stop and deliver your question to one person in the room.

GET RID OF FILLER WORDS

Filler words such as "um" and "err" can reduce the credibility of your message because they make you sound unsure about yourself. Speakers also use other, less obvious filler words, such as "like" and "so." The first step in reducing filler words is to become aware of the ones you use. The second step is to practice pausing when you are unsure of what to say. Most of the time, speakers use filler words because they don't know what to say next. If you practice deliberately pausing, you'll find that your filler words will naturally disappear.

You don't have to wait for your next speech or presentation to practice this technique. Use it during your everyday conversations. Practice pausing when you find yourself struggling with what to say next. It's difficult, but the more you do this, the easier it becomes.

GESTURE NATURALLY

One of the most common questions I hear as a public speaking coach is, "What should I do with my hands?"

You should try to use your hands as naturally as possible. Use your hands the way you normally would when having a conversation with a friend because that's really what public speaking is – it's a conversation with a group of friendly people who are interested in what you have to say.

For example, during his TED talk, Anthony Robbins (AkashKaria.com/Tony) asks the following question:

> "The question we've got to ask ourselves is: What is it? What is it that shapes us?"

When he asks this question, his right hand holds his chin in a thinking gesture. Was this a planned gesture? No, obviously not. It came naturally. The challenge for you is to become so passionate and so involved in your presentation that you stop thinking about your gestures and allow these natural gestures to pour out of you without consciously thinking about them.

Similarly, in his TED talk, Dan Pink uses gestures very effectively. When he talks about low, medium and high rewards, his hand starts off low to indicate low rewards, then rises to indicate medium rewards and rises even more to indicate high rewards. These gestures help show what Dan is saying.

Now, I realize that "gesture naturally" may not be a very helpful answer, so let me offer you some specifics as to how you should use your hands:

- **Don't cross your arms** – this signals to your audience that you are feeling defensive. Studies have revealed that people judge others who cross their arms as being less likeable and less friendly than those who do not.

- **Don't put your hands in your pockets** – there are two reasons why I would advise you not to do this. First, most people have a tendency to play about with the coins and other small items they have in their pockets. This can be really annoying. Second, your hands are a valuable tool in helping your audience see your story. You can use your hands to demonstrate shapes, divisions and sizes, so don't hide your hands!

- **Avoid the fig leaf** – The fig leaf is a posture many men tend to use. They fold hold their hands in front of their private parts. Not only can this be distracting, it also signals that the speaker feels unconfident and insecure.

- **Don't point at your audience** – Pointing your finger at your audience can be interpreted as rude and can offend your audience members. Instead, use an open palm to point at your audience if you have to.

- **Use your hands to show what you are saying** – Your hands should help bring your story alive for your audience. For example, if you say, "John was about six feet tall and built like a Greek statue", use your hands to show how tall and muscular he was.

USE POSTURE TO BRING YOUR CHARACTERS TO LIFE

When you are delivering your speech, make sure you stand in a confident posture. The most confident posture you can have is when you are standing with your back straight and your chest out. Confident speakers own the stage by using their bodies to take up as much space as they need. Speakers who are shy and nervous tend to adopt a small posture where they try to take up as little space as possible – they keep their head down and their hands close to their bodies to make themselves as tiny as possible.

I recommend that you videotape yourself speaking and analyze your body language to see whether you appear confident. When I did this exercise, I realized that I was slightly hunched over and wasn't standing fully straight. Since I have become aware of this, I have made a conscious decision to push my shoulders back further and make my back straight and erect. I know I'm doing it right because when I adopt this posture I feel more confident.

You can also bring your characters to life on stage by taking on their postures. For example, if one of the characters in your story is a tiny, frail old lady, you should assume her bent-over, tiny posture when delivering her dialogue. This helps your audience *see* your characters on stage.

KEEP YOUR FACIAL EXPRESSIONS CONGRUENT WITH YOUR STORY

Your facial expressions should be congruent with the story that you're telling. If you're delivering a very sad story, make sure that this sadness reflects on your face. If you're delivering a story where one of the characters in your speech is very excited, make sure that this excitement is evident on your face.

Your facial expressions can also help you get more laughs. When you are delivering a funny line, the right facial expression can help you get a bigger laugh. An open mouth depicting surprise, a raised eyebrow indicating confusion or wide eyes indicating fear can bring your story alive and make a line funnier. I encourage you to watch a video of one of your favorite comedians. Pay attention to his or her facial expressions and you will notice how facial expressions alone can sometimes trigger big belly laughs.

SHOW, DON'T TELL

Doug Stevenson, author of *The Story Theatre Method* says, "Behavior is language. Rather than saying, 'I was so frustrated I could hardly speak,' show what it looks and feels like. Be physically frustrated while you stammer and sputter to find the words to say." Whenever you can, follow the principle of showing rather than telling.

BIGGER AUDIENCE MEANS A BIGGER YOU

When you have a larger audience, you need an enlarged version of you.

This means that your gestures need to be larger and your voice needs to be louder. With a smaller audience, you don't need to be as loud.

For example, thousands of people line up to see the popular motivational speaker Anthony Robbins, so his gestures (and facial expressions) are always very large. However, during Tony's TED talk, his facial expressions and gestures were smaller because his audience was smaller.

MATCH THEIR ENERGY LEVEL

If you come across an audience with low energy, don't come out with high energy and expect your audience members to get equally excited. Instead, match their energy level and then lead them to a higher level of energy using activities, questions, etc. Similarly, when you come across audience members who are very excited and enthusiastic to see you, make sure you match that level of energy.

Audience members are always fired up for Anthony Robbins' seminars, so Tony comes out with a high level of energy and takes it up a notch. There's music, clapping, dancing.

However, during his TED talk, where audience members weren't as expressive with their emotions, Anthony Robbins came out with a much milder opening to match the energy level of his audience.

MAKE FULL USE OF THE STAGE

Avoid pacing back and forth on stage like a caged tiger because this can be distracting. Your movement on stage should be purposeful and should help show the story you are telling. I recommend that different scenes in your story should have their own spots on the stage. For example, if one of your scenes involves you at work, then you might set up that scene on the right side of the stage. Then, naturally, when you talk about going back home, you would walk to the left side of the stage where you would set up the scene at home. This way, when you walk back to the right side of the stage, your audience knows that you are back at the office without you having to say so. In this way, you can use the stage as a prop to make your story more visual for your audience.

You can also use the stage as a timeline. The left side of the stage (from the audience's perspective) would represent the past, center stage would represent the present and the right side of the stage would represent the future.

USE VOCAL VARIETY

Vocal variety refers to how you use your voice. You can use your voice to arouse different emotions in audience members. If you shorten your sentences, reduce your pauses and speak very quickly, you can create the excitement of a high-speed car chase. If you speak softly and at a leisurely pace while talking about a relaxing day at the beach, you can recreate the peacefulness of sitting at the beach.

The key to dynamic delivery, however, lies in the contrast. If you are always loud and fast, your audience members will soon get tired of listening to you because nothing stands out. If you speak quietly and softly, you will soon bore your audience into sleeping. The trick is to mix and match. Vary your volume and pace to create different moods for different scenes in your story.

When delivering character dialogue, vary your pitch. Take on the voice of your character – speak with a slightly deep voice when imitating a man and a slightly high voice when imitating a frail old woman. However, don't go overboard with this technique. If you're a man, you don't have to speak with a very high girlish voice when delivering a line by a little girl. Make the change subtle yet noticeable.

IN A NUTSHELL

Use the following tools to become a powerful and dynamic speaker

- Pause before you begin
- Smile
- Make eye contact
- Get rid of filler words
- Gesture naturally
- Use posture to bring your characters to life
- Keep facial expressions congruent with your story
- Show, don't tell
- Bigger audience means a bigger you
- Match the audience's energy level
- Make full use of the stage
- Use vocal variety

Chapter Twenty-Four

8 WAYS TO PREPARE FOR YOUR TED TALK

1. REHEARSE YOUR TALK

I'm a firm believer in rehearsing your speech in front of an audience. Gather your friends and family members so that you can feel what it will be like to deliver the speech when you have everyone's eyes focused on you. Your friends and family members will also be able to give you valuable insights regarding what needs to be changed or improved. You may want to join a Toastmasters club where you can practice your speech and get feedback from expert speakers.

If you are not able to rehearse your speech in front of an audience, then verbalize your speech. Lock yourself up in your room and deliver your speech the same way you would if you were in front of a live audience. This means that your volume, tone and gestures should be similar to what you would do on stage. If possible, try to videotape your rehearsal sessions so that you can review them later to see how you can improve.

2. EXERCISE

On the day of your speech, engage in some form of physical exercise. Go to the gym. Do some yoga. Go for a jog. Exercising will release endorphins, which will make you happier. You will feel less stressed and more confident about your presentation.

3. WALK AROUND THE ROOM

On the day of your speech, visit the room that you will be speaking in. Walk around the room so that you can get a feel of how clearly audience members will be able to see and hear you. As you walk around the room, check to make sure that there will be no objects blocking your audience's view of you when you are speaking on stage.

4. GET FAMILIAR WITH THE STAGE

Walk on the stage you will be speaking on. Familiarize yourself with how much room you have to move around. In addition, walking around on stage will put you into "speaking mode." It will get you into the right mindset to deliver a powerful presentation.

5. TEST THE EQUIPMENT

If you are going to be using PowerPoint or a microphone, check that it works. Test the microphone to ensure it doesn't make any screeching noises (due to electrical interference) as you walk around different parts of the room.

6. REHEARSE YOUR OPENING

Once again rehearse the opening of your speech. This way, when you get up on stage, you will find it easier to overcome any stage fright because you will already know what to say.

7. LISTEN TO MUSIC

Mark Hunter, the 2009 Toastmasters International World Champion of Public Speaking, told me that he would listen to some music right before his speech competitions. This helped keep him calm and focused.

Before your speech or presentation, listen to some of your favorite music. It can help you relax and focus.

8. VISUALIZE SUCCESS

World-class athletes visualize themselves delivering a world-class speech. This helps them "get in the zone."

Visualization can do wonders for you. Visualize yourself giving a great speech. Visualize yourself handling any unexpected challenges with ease. Visualization will get you "in the zone." It will get you mentally prepared for giving a great speech. It will make you feel confident and it will unconsciously prepare you for handling any unexpected challenges.

IN A NUTSHELL

Before you step up to the TED stage:

- Rehearse your talk
- Get some exercise to release endorphins
- Walk around the room you will be speaking in
- Get familiar with the stage
- Test the equipment
- Rehearse your opening
- Listen to music
- Visualize success

Chapter Twenty-Five

HOW TO DELIVER THE PERFECT TED TALK

So, what is the formula for delivering the perfect TED talk?

The perfect TED talk is simple, concrete, credible, contains an element of unexpectedness, arouses audience emotions and uses stories to drive home the message.

SIMPLE

- Find your core message
- Reduce your core message into a simple memorable Power Phrase
- Use a simple, easy-to-follow structure
- Provide a roadmap

UNEXPECTED

Avoid predictable, boring openings. Start with a story, question, quote, interesting/startling statement or a callback

- Use shocking statistics and facts
- Talk about something new
- Give the audience some unconventional piece of wisdom
- Argue against conventional wisdom
- Create a wow-moment

CONCRETE

- Be specific
- Turn abstract concepts such as failure into concrete images using metaphors, analogies, similes, case studies, examples and stories.
- Give the audience a concrete next step to take

CREDIBLE

- Borrow credibility from third-party quotes
- Build your credibility with your introduction

EMOTIONAL

- Address the elephant in the room
- Unite people towards a common goal
- Unite people towards a common enemy
- Build the we-connection
- Highlight the pain before offering a solution
- Use compelling visuals to arouse audience's emotions

- Arouse curiosity - tease before you tell
- Use humor to engage the audience's emotions

STORY

- Use the 5C's of storytelling
- Use the delivery techniques in Chapter twenty-three for dynamic storytelling

QUESTIONS OR COMMENTS?

I'd love to hear your thoughts. Email me at:
akash.speaker@gmail.com

NEED HELP?

I offer one-on-one coaching over Skype. I'll help you breathe life into your presentations. We'll work on your message, structure, opening, body, closing, humor, slides and presentation delivery. Reach me at akash.speaker@gmail.com

GRAB YOUR FREE EBOOKS

Thank you for buying this book. If you've enjoyed this book, you can grab $297 worth of free resources on how to become powerfully persuasive speaker by signing up for my email newsletter. When you sign up for my newsletter, you'll get more tools and techniques on how to breathe life into your presentations. Join over 7,900 of your peers and receive free, exclusive content that I don't share on my blog. Sign up on: www.AkashKaria.com/FREE

YOU MIGHT ALSO LIKE...

If you enjoyed this book, you will love my book, "How to Design TED-Worthy Presentation Slides". It contains advanced tools, tips and techniques on how to design sexy presentation slides that breathe life into your presentations instead of draining it away from your audience. Buy it at: www.AkashKaria.com/TEDWorthy

ABOUT THE AUTHOR

Akash Karia is an award winning speaker and communication skills trainer who has been ranked as one of the Top Ten speakers in Asia Pacific. He has won over forty public speaking championships, including the prestigious title of 2012 Hong Kong Champion of Public Speaking. He is an in-demand international speaker who has spoken to a wide range of audiences including bankers in Hong Kong, students in Tanzania and yoga teachers in Thailand. He currently lives in Tanzania where he leads the sales team of a multi-million dollar company.

"If you want to learn presentation skills, public speaking or just simply uncover excellence hidden inside of you or your teams, **Akash Karia is the coach to go to**" - Raju Mandhyan, TV show host, Expat Insights, Philippines

"Akash Karia is a fine public speaker who knows his subject very well. He has an immense understanding in what it takes for a successful presentation to pull through. A rare talent who **has much in store for you as an individual, and better yet, your organization.**" - Sherilyn Pang, Business Reporter, Capital TV, Malaysia

Akash is available for speaking engagements and flies from Tanzania. Contact him for coaching and training through his website: www.AkashKaria.com

OTHER BOOKS BY THE AUTHOR

HOW TO DESIGN TED-WORTHY PRESENTATION SLIDES

How to Design TED-Worthy Presentation Slides is a short, practical and step-by-step guide to creating sexy slides.

It is based on an extensive analysis of some of the best TED speakers, such as Brene Brown, Daniel Pink, Amy Cuddy, Larry Lessig, Seth Godin, Bill Gates and many, many more.

Included in the book are sample sexy slides from TED talks, as well as from across the web, to help you master the art of presentation design. Get the book here: www.AkashKaria.com/TEDWorthy

STORYTELLING TECHNIQUES FOR ELECTRIFYING PRESENTATIONS

Master the art of public speaking by mastering the art of storytelling. This short book analyzes the speeches and stories of four world-class speakers and shows you how you too can create stories that keep your audiences captivated. Get the book on here: www.AkashKaria.com/Story

SHARE YOUR MESSAGE

Thank you for buying this book. I am passionate about helping others becoming better public speakers. My ambition is to help ten thousand people master the art of public speaking so that they can, in turn, can help others. So if you've found value from this book, please pass this book onto a friend so that together we can eliminate boring presentations. Please also consider leaving a review on Amazon: http://amzn.to/ZJ9VLv

One important principle in public speaking is that you should end your speech with a bang! End in a memorable way. End with a clear next step for your audience to follow, which is why I'm going to end this book with one final and important application exercise. I encourage you to do this exercise before any speech or presentation because it will put you into a confident mind-set.

I want you to relax, sit back and imagine yourself up on stage, sharing your message with your audience. Imagine the participants smiling and enthusiastic. Imagine them being hooked onto your every word. Imagine them totally engaged in your speech. Imagine them laughing at the humor in your speech. Imagine them spellbound by your stories. Imagine yourself enthusiastic, confident and enjoying the moment.

Use all the senses – Visual, Auditory, Kinesthetic and Smell – to make the scene come alive in your mind. Hear your audience laughing. See them smiling. Hear the applause. See yourself succeeding.

Now go deliver a great TED Talk. Share your message with world. And let me know how it goes.

Akash

Made in the USA
Lexington, KY
21 December 2016